WORD SIGHTINGS

MAJOR LITERARY AUTHORS
VOLUME 12

STUDIES IN
MAJOR LITERARY AUTHORS
OUTSTANDING DISSERTATIONS

edited by
William E. Cain
Wellesley College

A ROUTLEDGE SERIES

Other Books in This Series:

WORD SIGHTINGS
Poetry and Visual Media in Stevens, Bishop, and O'Hara

Sarah Riggs

ROUTLEDGE
NEW YORK & LONDON

Published in 2002 by
Routledge
29 West 35th Street
New York, NY 10001
www.Routledge-ny.com

Published in Great Britain by
Routledge
11 New Fetter Lane
London EC4P 4EE
www.routledge.com

Routledge is a member of the Taylor & Francis Group.

Excerpts from COLLECTED POEMS by Frank O'Hara, copyright © 1971 by Maureen Granville-Smith, Administratix of the Estate of Frank O'Hara. Used by permission of Alfred A. Knopf, a division of Random House, Inc.

Excerpts from THE COMPLETE POEMS: 1927–1979 by Elizabeth Bishop. Copyright © 1979, 1983 by Alice Helen Methfessel. Reprinted by permission of Farrar, Straus and Giroux, LLC.

Excerpts from THE COLLECTED POEMS OF WALLACE STEVENS by Wallace Stevens, copyright © 1954 by Wallace Stevens and renewed 1982 by Holly Stevens. Used by permission of Alfred A. Knopf, a division of Random House, Inc.

10 9 8 7 6 5 4 3 2 1

Library of Congress Cataloging-in-Publication Data

Riggs, Sarah, 1971–
  Word sightings : poetry and visual media in Stevens, Bishop, and
O'Hara / by Sarah Riggs.
    p. cm. — (Studies in major literary authors ; v. 12)
Includes bibliographical references (p.) and index.
  ISBN 0-415-93859-7 (hardback)
  1. American poetry—20th century—History and criticism. 2. Vision in literature.
3. Literature and technology—United States—History—20th century. 4. Mass media
and literature—United States—History—20th century. 5. Art and literature—United
States—History—20th century. 6. Stevens, Wallace, 1879–1955—Criticism and
interpretation. 7. Bishop, Elizabeth, 1911–1979—Criticism and interpretation.
8. O'Hara, Frank—Criticism and interpretation. 9. Visual perception in literature.
10. Mass media in literature. 11. Art in literature. I. Title. II. Series.
  PS310.V57 R54 2002
  811'.509—dc21

                                                                    2002004220

Printed on acid-free, 250 year-life paper
Manufactured in the United States of America

Contents

Acknowledgments

The kinship and conversation of Julia Carlson, Stacy Doris, Troy Gordon, Wendy Riggs, Rei Terada, Marjorie Levinson, and above all, Tim Bahti, have carried this book through to fruition.

I also want to thank Melanie Cooley, Bonnie Costello, Victoria Duckett, Maria Gough, Gia Hamilton, Kerry Larson, Brenda Laws, Dominique Leherpeur, Michael Palmer, Robert Riggs, Susanna Ryan, Cole Swensen, Jon Thompson, and Jennifer Vetter.

I am grateful to the Mellon Foundation and to the University of Michigan's English Department for granting assistance during stages of this work.

Introduction

Paired together, do poetry and technology form a paradox? A number of the features of post-industrial modernity are anathema to what readers have traditionally valued in Western poetry. Technological growth as we know it thrives on mass consumption over unique expression, on rapid human adaptation to its features, and on an emphasis on the value of the practical over the beautiful; it alters space, human contact, perception, and rapidly renders obsolete work methods, objects, and modes of expression. American poetry, for its part, has attracted the largest number of readers for its elevation of the individual apart, its values of beauty, the pastoral, natural response, and emotive refuge in language. The clash between an undeterred mass phenomenon and an art form with a long elite tradition is obvious. What is less obvious is how peculiar the situation of poetry is. Of the multitude of arts that flourish in twentieth-century America, not only the visually-dominated media arts that are direct products of technological innovation, like cinema and photography, benefit from its development; also, painting, music, drama, sculpture, i.e., the refined classical arts, are transformed by their technological components and extensions. Painting, which will never be the same as a result of its mechanical reproduction—the idea Walter Benjamin introduces with wounded recognition of the original painting's loss of aura[1]—can also be inflected positively: "Painting will never be the same!" How astonishing, joyful, that Americans, few of whom live within close range of a cathedral, can see art nearly firsthand, in catalogues, postcards, posters, and all other reproduction outlets. This commercialization and mass-access boost the growth of most of the creative arts, including music (radios, music players, electronic amplification, and so forth). Further, most of the arts undergo a technological hybridization that is an additional boon because of the seepage of new techniques, materials, and processes that vitalize and update their classical media.

For poetry, its pronounced technological components are print technology and circulation, advances which, though once revolutionary, and in an ongoing state of flux, have been nothing new for a long time. Though the impact of the worldwide web remains to be seen, for American poets at mid-century the revivification that many of the other arts experience within the very modes of art-making leaves them out of the loop. Why is this not true for artists in all text-based genres? Essayists and theorists, many of whom have emerged as prime artist-thinkers of our time—Benjamin among them, as well as Martin Heidegger, Georg Simmel, Theodor Adorno, Roland Barthes, Gilles Deleuze and Michel Foucault—and many others, have schooled us in the social impact of technology. Theirs is a text-medium that thrives on technology as theme, in however resistant a mode, elevating prose critique to a level of pleasure and intellectual fascination amply evident in advanced Western university curricula. But if the prose essay is the best prepared of literary forms to discuss technology outright, poetry is surely the least.

Reductive though it may be, the point needs underscoring that poetry, as exemplified by the short, dense lyric, is not like other literary genres, and it is not like other genres because of its staunch refusal to privilege the referent. The existence of an object, say, a Cadillac, has less significance, and metaphorically speaking, less reality for the poet, than the language by which one relates to a Cadillac, the subjective private experience that conjures and responds to the very word "Cadillac." Common association dictates that novels are about plot and characters, essays about ideas, and biographies about people, and no matter how modern writing and theory play havoc with these categories, they nonetheless retain a minimal pertinence as points of departure. Poetry can have any or all of these elements, but what makes it poetry is its refusal to really be *about* something—the thing, that which is referenced, is less important, just really not the point, because the point is an emotion, and a way of finding an alternative language to express that emotion. Gertrude Stein's turn-of-the-century test case, *Tender Buttons*, relishes making this point, showing off the poetic as a state of extreme play in which the signposts of reference, manipulated as such and, to the extent possible, nothing more, set off an array of feelings—amusement, frustration, surprise, delight, bewilderment.[2] Readers are hard-pressed to say what the writing is about, save for the discrete emotions that accompany the recognition that it was *not* about a box, Mildred's umbrella, rhubarb, salad dressing and an artichoke, despite the particular sub-headings.

Stein's exercise is subversive. So too is the work of the American poets I undertake to expose in this book as writers who have not previously been understood as vitally engaged in an ambivalent clutch with technology. Paradox or no, poetry and technology unavoidably mesh, and the American poet, responding to the emotional pulse of the present, not that of centuries past, knows it. My contention is that the American poet turns depletion into resource, and converts the disadvantage of technological lack into a primary focus. The array of eloquent, often self-disguised, responses to modern life that arise out of competition with technology, ranging from text-defensive poetic effects to image-envious conceits, have a pertinence that is unavailable to any other art. Working against a set of limitations never before so imposing, the American poet pivots on an idiosyncratic vantage point; attentive, alienated, possessing heightened tools for responding to lack, she and he search the far edges of poetic language in the attempt to create uniquely poetic experience. The desired result is a set of effects that are potentially more meaningful for their lacks than any artistic advantage gained by technology could achieve.

Of these poetic effects, some mimic technological effects as precisely as possible, ranging from Elizabeth Bishop's interestingly failed efforts at optically precise imagery to Frank O'Hara's quasi-3-D certainty of physical presence. These self-constructed methods of outshining technology, as well as their flip side, Wallace Stevens' construction of an image-resistant language reality, have much to teach about how the new realities posed by technological advance crucially lack the capacity to comment upon their own procedures as they occur. Language, and poetic language in particular, according to the claim I take these poets implicitly to be making, can enact the failures and incompletions of technology as experiences in themselves worth lingering over and digesting, in a way that technology and hybrid media cannot.

On one level, the poets' scraped-together mode of survival is very American, stemming from a nation composed of the dispossessed, the poor, the fanatical, who seek to tame what is unconquerable and manage to overcome against the odds. At another level, it is out of step with America, because the majority of the populace, the poets included, have much to gain from the fast-developing object-oriented advances that technology proffers. They have little choice, at any rate, but to make the best of the new momentum, and the biographies of American poets reveal that indulgence in city life, modern means of transportation, modes of popular pleasure, were embraced by even the most prim of aesthetes (even Marianne Moore rode the subways). It is worth considering in this context how the Western construction of the poet, inherited and adapted as it has been by Americans, has long presented the poet as the idiosyncratic outsider, the sage out of step with the masses, the Thoreau-like creature looking into ponds. Robert Frost, over decades America's most popular poet, offers the gift of inclusion in this exalted pastoral terrain of exclusion: "in the rush of everything to waste," Frost writes to his readers in the 1930s, ". . . you may have the power of standing still—."[3] Though technology may look like a threat to nature, specifically poetry as identified with the natural, the opposite turns out to be true. Modernity, rather than undermining the currency of the poet, turns out to be a great boon. Counterintuitive as it may be, this is a prime moment for the American poet because the threat technology poses can be self-adopted, worked to advantage.

How does this work? Americans who gravitate to the unusual career of poet do so because they seek to empower their personal, alienated, emotive response to events—to draw subjective feelings more closely in line with external contexts. And what could be more alienating, what could throw things more out of whack with feelings, as Heidegger claims of mechanized false proximity, than technology?[4] A primary reason American poetry takes off in the twentieth century, I contend, is its empowered position at the margin. A Romantic subject position is now concretized, walled in exile, by potent objects and technical apparatuses with which the poet does not participate. Though any modern poet of integrity destabilizes Heidegger's elitist claim for poetic authenticity, the view of poetry as the exemplary stay against the contingent, particulate assault of the post-industrial sphere of things is nonetheless an indispensable point of departure.

Waves of generations of American poets of massive talent and extensive contribution attest to how well the equation has worked. Anyone so inclined can come up with a list of American poets, and though to do so invokes a canon, it also shows how abundant any list would be. The first generation of modernists poets born in the 1870s and 1880s can include Stein, Stevens, William Carlos Williams, Ezra Pound, H.D., Marianne Moore, T.S. Eliot, and a second generation born at the turn of the century and the 1910s, Laura Riding, Hart Crane, Louis Zukofsky, Charles Olson, Bishop, Robert Hayden, John Berryman, Robert Lowell. Another wave comes of age in the postwar period, among them Denise Levertov, James Merrill, Allen Ginsberg, O'Hara, John Ashbery, and Sylvia Plath. Among poets now reaching maturity in the written tradition (performance poets are excluded, because their reliance on amplified voice and physical gesture considerably diminishes media angst), a generation of poets involved in language experimentation includes Lyn Hejinian, Michael Palmer, Susan Howe, and Mei-mei Berssenbrugge—writers who are pushing poetry to radical edges that render fresh the drive to destabilize the world of things in a uniquely linguistic way. The younger generations of poets are by no means diluting the project, but extending the language experiment in attuned, often comic, directions, apparent in journals such as *The Germ, Fence, Raddle Moon,* and *Verse.*

In short, American poetry is very much alive. It may be that the large-scale American indifference to poetry as something learned in school, obviously less interesting than cinema or popular music, as opposed to the cultural respect for the art form evident in much of Europe, forces American poets out of a false sense that poetry can circle back within first-tier modernist aesthetics. The necessity that prompted Charles Baudelaire in "The Painter and Modern Life" to redefine the artist's role is one that

Americans continue to feel anew.[5] The cost of trying to accentuate the poet as self-constructed rescuer of a potentially doomed medium, however, and along with it, a mode of expression felt by each individual as somehow crucial to survival, is considerable. The narrow chance of survival in the face of unlikely efforts to recuperate loss, lack, absence, and to convert what is *not* there through self-fashioned language-acts, goes against the grain. Waves of postwar suicides among American poets may or may not attest to the tenuous position; certainly Charles Altieri's impression that poetry may be becoming more and more desperate[6] is one that underscores an ongoing sense of crisis which each individual poem works to dissolve but of course never does.

Part of the issue is that technology is not oblique in the way poetry is, at least insofar as emotions are concerned. It forces into question all those categories handed to the post-Romantic poet by tradition: the individual, beauty, personal expression, nature, direct observation, a calm inner-human core, a creative (not consumer) impulse, the validity of mourning and of subjective response. Modernity, for which this book's synecdoche is technology, and more narrowly, visual media, requires the poet to recuperate, alter, morph, and adjust these categories in the face of inward and outward resistance. That technological developments stimulate the emotions in active ways has as its side-effect that modern individuals crave an understanding of the agitation, excitement, or what recent perceptual history names "attention," a series of positive, brief states of intense absorption.[7] This book isolates discrete cases in which poets position themselves at an intersection with other media, thereby giving an emotional history of technology, and addressing readers who feel themselves to suffer marginalization from all those values mentioned above. I develop a set of quirky reading strategies to keep up with the poets' inventive, often illogical and anomalistic, methods for the uphill work of recuperating a potentially outmoded role, and converting what is threatened most acutely—poetic language—into a resource.

THE CRITICAL CONTEXT

How does one arrive at this book's approach, so illogically founded on paradox? By the recognition that the paradox as such, adopted by poets, philosophers and critics alike, is not wholly, but to large extent, a construction perpetuated to suit certain ends and expectations. That poetry and technology form a paradox is a significant idea, and is constitutive of many poetic aesthetics, but can only in one part be substantiated with empirical evidence. This part, that poetry has a low percentage of actual sensory content and a high percentage of imaginary sensory content, rarifies poetry in the Hegelian tradition to the *ne plus ultra* of artistic expression. The genre represents for Hegel the overcoming, the mastery, of sensuousness, itself associated with a base reliance upon external conditions. This line of thought, extended as well as complicated by twentieth-century theorists such as Adorno, logically preserves a sphere for the classical arts as apart from popular media. Early film theory is one of the players in undermining Hegel's hierarchy by contending that cinema, rather than in paradoxical opposition to art, counts as an art form. Perhaps it is not surprising that poetry has not had an equivalent spokesperson to Rudolf Arnheim, author of *Film as Art*,[8] to underscore that poetry is as much an art form as cinema. It has been safer, and more useful, to assume that poetry is the winner in the paradox war, and that it goes without saying that poetry is a superior art. The medium has long been positioned as aesthetic escape, a hermetic pleasure separated off from what is uncomfortable or least tenable about encroaching realities.

This positioning takes some effort, if, as I contend, no American poet is *not* writing about technology in the twentieth century. Especially by mid-century, technology is too pervasive and determinative of the emotional pulse of a nation that is by any count, many generations deep into post-industrial modernity. The majority of American poetry critics, however, including those of the present day, exclude technology from their discussions. This stance remains possible because—and this observation is crucial to the reading method I develop—of the willfully mysterious methods of American poets: strains of postwar poets fabricate individual sets of tricks by which to bely readers (and to some extent themselves) as to what actually is being addressed. In the late 1940s and the 1950s, few American poets raise technology to a central theme named outright as such. This is brazen, stubborn, seemingly backward. Not to write about film, cars, radios, airplanes, factories, the atom bomb, when they are making such a racket, is an audacious thing to do—and not, finally, possible. But it *is* possible to disguise emotions about them in other things—birch trees, boats, trysts, hallucinations, travel—in the vein of the romantic pastoral. In short, the poetry miscues. It substitutes referents. Who will articulate an overwhelming set of emotions about the particular destruction of Hiroshima, tell us how to feel about something so unfamiliar, so awful, that we lack the words for it? It just may be a poet writing about a fish.

This is odd. But it is not a grave betrayal, since the referent is not the point, not really. The work being done, of bringing external events and things more closely in line with feelings, may perhaps best be done through something the poet is familiar with—that is, something minimally beautiful, natural. Readers fall for it every time because we are gullible, rendered passive from a lifelong training in common sense: told to believe we are reading about a fish being caught, we believe. Told to read about a jar in Tennessee, we still believe, moreorless. American readers, even full-time readers, have been slow to assimilate the elements of modern life into aesthetic experience, to think, for instance, of poetry and technology as contiguous. The self-obscuring tactics of the American poet at once play into and disturb these resistances. Alongside every avant-garde artist in modern America, from Alfred Stieglitz to Andy Warhol, the poet has also been involved, despite self-advertisements to the contrary, in a reflexive diffusion of categorical distinctions between expressive media, and a redefinition of what makes up current aesthetics.

Due mostly to the ambivalence of figures such as T.S. Eliot, who with one hand cuts through modernity with a harsh, appealing lexicon in *The Wasteland* (1922), and with the other canonizes, setting up poetry as very high in the essays of the 1940s and 1950s,[9] the gritty vein in American poetry has been slow to take off. The embrace of the city, the vulgar, the low, as viable themes, explored in this book via O'Hara, does not enter conceptions of poetry at large prior to say, Allen Ginsberg. Other prominent poets alongside Eliot, such as Pound, Frost, and Stevens, are similarly engaged in deep internal struggles over high and low; Robert Lowell perpetuates the bi-polar legacy. Zukofsky, E.E.Cummings, and some of the poets coming more into the limelight such as Charles Reznikoff, Jean Toomer, Langston Hughes, and George Oppen, help shake up what is possible in poetic discourse.

The manipulation of the myth of being out of step with the time certainly wins the approval of critics, as tricks, whether genuinely duplicitous or merely effective guises, feed into rather than clog the gears of the American institutional machine that in the 1950s and 60s would continue to churn out a hermetic image of the poet. Even now, it seems absurd to turn to the poet for insight into technological experience, when the poet represents, and often emphasizes, the idealized refusal to give into change. Technology as a subject of academic interest more logically surfaces in Film Theory and Cultural Studies. Alternatively, New Historicism, Gender Studies, and Postcolonialism each offer links to culture that bypass the hermetic sphere assigned to poetry since New Criticism and Deconstruction, however brilliantly, dead-ended for a time the possibilities for poetry critique to include culture in the conversation.

Poetry by and large has been excluded from cutting-edge dialogues in American academic circles since the late 1980s, and this state of exile has not induced the positive, productive fruits that it has for American poets, rather a state of blank and of diminishing numbers. A persistent and stubborn refusal to separate poetry from high aesthetics has sorely marginalized poetry from the theoretical discourses of the 1990s, even as the surge in creative interest reaches new heights. Unprecedented numbers of American college graduates want to write poetry, a tiny number want to study it: the conditions are primed for the creative impulse, at a low for the critical one. Interestingly, one approach to revive poetry in recent years grows out of Jerome McGann's emphasis on the technological component of writing, its material contexts, and the iconics of the page.[10] This vein of study remains peripheral for the reasons stated above; with notable exceptions such as

Stéphane Mallarmé and Laura Riding, most poets are not sufficiently enamored with the material mechanics of their medium to make it crucial to the workings of their poetry. For a visual artist such as Jackson Pollock, the materiality and expressive features of the art form easily merge because the sensuous component of painting is more prominent for painting than it is for poetry. The sensuous lack that marks the poetic medium means that conversations about the iconic page hover around poetry in fascinating ways, tangents of great intrigue, but ultimately do not have the force to redeem poetry as a pertinent, primary source.

The earliest important exception to technology-resistant trends in poetry criticism, Majorie Perloff's *Radical Artifice: Writing Poetry in the Age of Media* (1991),[11] is significant for several reasons: its extended sense of media influences as including television, advertising, and computers; its breadth of treatment of contemporary experimental writers; its account of media as multi-sensory rather than specifically visual; its appreciation of the poems as stylistic registers of cultural change. Perloff removes taboos about interart comparisons, as well as high- and low-associations, that enable readers to consider cultural media as not only significant, but as inevitable, tools for poetic interpretation. The principal disappointment of the approach is that the bulk of critical energy goes into reconfiguring who the new players and media are, rather than into showing what is radical at the level of language. In short, Perloff's method gets clogged in referents rather than in showing what poets are doing with reference, a familiar problem to poetry criticism. Perloff's book-length study of Frank O'Hara, an early foray into interdisciplinary criticism, likewise does marvelous work to establish the painterly context in which O'Hara thrived, and falls short of new methods for reading O'Hara's highly experimental oeuvre. Perhaps these deficiencies at the level of close reading, a tool which after all is the principal inheritance of hermetic critics, can explain Perloff's stance vis-à-vis Stevens in "Revolving in Crystal," an essay eschewed by partisans of Stevens for its politial critique of the poetry he wrote during the war.[12] Though Stevens merits some critique for being unremittingly cryptic, Perloff's culture-policing grows out of a failure to read the shuddering level of engagement Stevens' poetry registers with the contemporary world.

Carrie Noland's *Poetry at Stake: Lyric Aesthetics and the Challenge of Technology* (1999)[13] addresses the massive influence of mechanization precisely through the kind of close reading required, and is the best book in the emerging field of cultural poetry critique. Noland's tactic emphasizes the technological component of writing in exposing modern French poets, and contemporary mixed-media American artists, as already imbricated in industrial advance. The method is viable, and the readings work to expose a poetics as ambivalent as that of Char, whom Noland shows as split between Heideggerean rarification and the mock-literary encoding of wartime radio messages. Noland's emphasis on the technological component contributes to overturning the polarized status of poetry and technology, and in this respect advances aims shared by this book. In jumping over the text-based American poet, and in the decision to emphasize poetry as a technology, however, Noland misses the strongest argument for the dissolution of high-low distinctions, and for why poetry matters to modernity. This is that technological lack is the poet's principal tool for altering attitudes about language art, and the great mobilizer for producing stunning poetic effects. Another important addition to the field is Michael Davidson's *Ghostlier Demarcations: Modern Poetry and the Material Word* (1997), which works to define literary materiality in the poetics of Stein, Zukofsky, Howe, Anderson, and others, as historically layered into the text documents themselves, and therefore implicated in social critique.[14] The bulk of scholarship that elucidates the question at hand, however, must be borrowed from other disciplines, principally from the study of visual art, for reasons I will now explain.

AGE OF THE IMAGE

The technological trump card of the twentieth century is the reproduction of the image because of its overt claim to witness and present the real. Visual media's mesmerizing evolutions, from black and white images into color moving pictures, by no means quantitatively dominate technological innovation, but they do place an imperative on denotation, and on the image as its marker. The new visual media also force the question of denotation in art. Barthes' writings provide important underpinnings for the current book because he explores not only how denotative certainty is brought to a crisis by the rise of photo-realism, but also what that means for literature. In "The Reality Effect," Barthes discusses the convergence of an Aristotelian mimetic tradition, in which art purports to mirror the real, with a historical, technical tradition, in which art is eclipsed by function. The tense hybridity of these two traditions corresponds in literature, in Barthes' model, to the production of seemingly hyper-concrete details, or reality effects.[15]

The paradox of mimesis and technical function is the very paradox I explore here as one of poetry and technology. Poetry arises out of a mimetic tradition; technology out of a functional one. But again, how to talk about two terms seemingly so estranged? Art theory does most of the groundbreaking work for the obvious reason that each primarily visual art already contains a significant marker of modern day function: the image. Photorealistic images are the rapid touchstones of events, the witnesses of history more indisputable than verbal accounts. Visual markers of function, from microscopes to postcards, underscore as does each visual technology, a momentary impression that vision is the definitive measure of experience.

The modern hierarchy of the senses empowers vision at the top, setting off a series of battles against the tyranny of sight that is arguably the defining feature of twentieth-century art. Though conceptions of vision as the most despotic sense are centuries old, and ocular perspective an inheritance from the Renaissance, for the moderns, it is the penetration of vision into mechanized society that makes sight into a new kind of challenge. The modern artist enters a fully fledged struggle with photorealism, producing works as far afield as the readymade and abstract painting. Theories of art have responded seriously to understanding this challenge by exploring material practices that challenge the hypostatization of the visual, including Duchamp's concept of anti-retinality, the Russian Formalists' pursuit of phonic and graphic palpability, Pollock's shift to horizontal, conceptual art, and myriad other experiments with alternative sensory art. But even as the battle gets waged as one between the senses, as between tactility and ocularity, the clash between the senses is a displacement of a larger clash, one in which artists and poets both have the largest stake, between art and function.

Just as there is no simple divide between artistic creation and objective reportage, the relation between art and function is a complex one; the art term is incessantly borrowing from, copying, merging with, not to say undermining, the function term. Art criticism shows, as poetry criticism does not, that modern art is always borrowing from function. A Duchamp door, according to Rosalind Krauss, is "a kind of optical machine through which it is impossible *not* to see."[16] Art does what machines do, but it strips away the function. In other words, a work of modern art acts like an optical machine, but differently. And its lack of function acts as a critique of the technical object's excessive functionality.

This logic applies to modern poetry, but is harder to grasp because the stripping away of function is not visibly apparent. Poetry, because largely immaterial, and lacking the sensuous content of the visual arts, is reduced to producing an abstraction of an abstraction. There is no Duchamp door in poetry because the medium cannot display a situation in which "it is impossible *not* to see." In poetry, the opposite is always the case: it is impossible *to* see. Thus the modern poet is in the clutches of a strange contradiction: how to display an excess of sight in a medium in which there is none at all. Paradoxically, it is technology that offers some ideas. Benjamin writes in "Little History of Photography" how photography, with its devices of slow motion and enlargement, reveals the secrets of the optical unconscious.[17] The modern individual not only sees differently, and sees more, but in some cases sees more artistically: the patterns of signage in a Walker Evans photograph, the tenuous dimensionality of a stereoscopic view of Paris, a dreamlike state in a Murnau film. Fantastic, unthinkable ways of seeing—what the poet-visionary has experimented with all along—now are concretized by technology into actual imagery.

Critical writers who work on both the visual arts and textual theory such as Johanna Drucker, James Elkins, Michael Fried, Martin Jay, W.J.T. Mitchell, and Naomi Schor lead the way in making new art phenomena and anti-realist ways of thinking about vision available for literary study as well. Fried examines the territory between the painter and self-portrait as one of self-writing and of slippage between visible and bodily legibility. Locating a tension between traditional mimetic function and the desire for corporeal merger in the self-portraits of Henri Fantin-Latour, he underscores the two extremes at play: a realism of eyesight versus a realism of the body. The fascination with paint, bits of brushhair, the placement of an ink bottle at the edge of the canvas, in his analysis, are invitations into materiality. Mimetic function in art collapses with something more elusive because more tactile, an exploration of the contours of the artistic medium as a counter-response to the functionality, and the excess of ocular realism, in modern life.[18] In *What Painting Is*, Elkins inquires into the obsessions with paint *qua* paint, not trained to mimic an object, but for its textures, pigments, and viscous qualities. He examines progressive acts of mixing, literally, with the medium, as paint marks first the artist's skin, then the clothes, then the very furniture of the painter's physical surroundings.[19]

The keyword to interpreting the analogous attractions to materiality in that least material of mediums, and that least referential of genres, poetry, is ekphrasis. Defined as the verbal representation of a visual representation, ekphrasis is the traditional mode in which poetry relates to visual art, dating back to Homer's writings on Achilles' shield. Because ekphrasis has an extensive historical lineage, and because it stages the intersection of poetry with the visual, it is a useful concept for seeing how the modern poet parts ways with mimesis, and with static ocular conceptions of the work of art. Since the mimetic stranglehold is powerful, most critics of poetry and painting look for likeness, and limit the work of art to classical models. Mitchell helpfully exposes the visual-verbal relation as by no means one of simple complementarity, but as fraught with eroticism and vying for power, in instances ranging from British Romantic ekphrasis to Stevens' "Anecdote of a Jar."[20]

Pushing Mitchell's work a step further, I situate ekphrasis as a power struggle at a historical moment when the definition of visual representation is up for grabs. What would it mean for poetry, not to mime cinema, surely a pathetically failing endeavor, but to vie for power with it? The terms of the text-image wars have been too limited thus far, restricted to vertical frame painting and single poem responses. What if a whole poetic oeuvre is construed as a response to the representational modes of a visual medium? Further, what if this response is not adulatory, but seeks an avenue for poetry in which its efforts at material effects rival in fascination, say, Pollock's paint?

Such questions led to my idea to use the mechanical apparatuses of twentieth-century image reality as hinges for reading poetry, and for understanding poetry as a response to, and commentary on, technological modes of representation. The postcard, the optic machine, the moving picture—each provides a departure point for the poets in this study to engage on a poetic critique of sight, and to question visual denotation as the primary marker of experience. Each acts as a reference point in the struggle with denotation in the poet's own territory, language. And each points to the technological backdrop that impels the poet to lend emotive import to denotative break-down.

PARAGONE

The American poet responds to the handicap of sensory lack much as a blind person develops a more highly attuned sense of hearing, and a more responsive sense of touch. Placing her or himself at the precipice of the technical image, the poet develops an acute vocabulary for sensory depletion, and compensates for poetry's double lack of function as neither technological nor visual with a stunning array of reality effects. The paragone for this book, three poets of successive generations responding to visual media primarily during the postwar years, could hardly be more different in their creative responses to the challenge. A biographical focus on the poets at mid-century shows Wallace Stevens in the summer in New Haven "surviving" on postcards from Europe, Elizabeth Bishop grinding binocular lenses in the Navy's optical factory in Key West, and Frank O'Hara getting "two more lousy movies under [his] belt" in Manhattan after an evening at the opera.[21] These biographical details, minor bit parts of the poet's lives, expose the instances when the encounter with technical visual media is, however narrowly, chosen rather than imposed. Which discrete aspects of a massive phenomenon so threatening to poetry at large could attract, fascinate, and compel these poets? And how did what the poets find in postcards, in optics, in film, seep into and alter the kind of poetry they wrote?

These are the material clues from which the reading method proceeds, and the research stops there; historical context is not the aim of this book, but an understanding of how poetry *reads* culture is. To do this, I follow the poets' leads, which is to say the lines and words of the poetry. The degree of proximity, of reading close-up, is necessitated by the fact that the poets are anything but simple, direct, transparent, and function-oriented in their methods of communication. Each lives up to the role of the American poet as the sage apart, launching off from a savage lack, and surmounting challenge by self-made works of linguistic difficulty. The poems are rife with ambivalence, paradox, vacillations between media-effacement and aggrandizement, obsessions with the shortcomings of poetry, and convoluted passions for what poetry can do that nothing else can.

The poets in this study have in common what all twentieth-century American poets have in common. They pull verbal effects as from a Troubadour's bag of tricks to woo absence into presence, by accentuating tropes such as puns, similes, metaphor, paradox and chiasmus. The result is a kind of hyper-poetry, an excess of poem, that depends upon drawing attention to how the faculty of seeing in poetry is sightless. But the individual poetic results are quite different, and represent wildly different critiques of visual culture. Though the three poets selected here are chosen partly for being from successive generations—for the difference being seventy, forty-five, or thirty years old makes in responding to a rapidly developing cultural phenomenon—the choice more importantly stems from the diversity of responses to a common paradox. That is to say that even as the work on Stevens perhaps could be achieved out of a similar study on Stein or Riding, or the work on Bishop achieved through Moore or Williams or Swenson, my feeling is that the results do not merely rely upon the discrete examples, the primary texts at hand; the poems *are* the findings.

The self-constructed nature of the American poet's critique of photorealism makes the kind of reality effects attempted in the poems peculiar to Stevens, peculiar to Bishop, and peculiar to O'Hara. In Stevens, we see the attempt to evacuate language of sight: poetry acts as the absence of any sense, the fabled sixth sense. Sites of impasse, staged by the postcard, force entry by the sidedoor into language reality. Poetic language becomes a safe, exclusive terrain of invention, but even as Stevens is the most hermetic of the three poets, his aesthetic revolves most acutely around the problem of what he refuses to allow in. When Stevens makes impossible claims to vicarious travel through receiving postcards, I follow the peculiar logic to explore how place names acquire a reality for Stevens apart from the places themselves. Denotation acts as a key to unlocking Stevens' work, for he is the poet closest to the beginnings of articulating the problem of photorealism for the American poet.

Positioned as the centerpiece of this project, Bishop gives the most literal and transparent articulation of the problem. Her poetry mimes the optically enhanced eye, and reenacts the problem of seeing too much. Points of visual-verbal contact are nothing but the products of tropes in the poems; Bishop would pass them off as real sites by invoking all manner of visual illusions and frames, as staged by fleeting references to postcards, the camera obscura, the stereoscope, magnifying glasses, microscopes, and binoculars. Bishop's insistence on optic denotation acts as a kind of excessive functionalism that the poems cannot support. By staging literal contact, and its failure, Bishop's writing produces a figurative bonus that, in turn, seems real. These effects, examined in conjunction with Barthes' work in the final section of the Bishop chapter, provide a lucid example of eye-as-truth reality effects.

O'Hara is the most at ease with the contradictions of seeing, and thus the most equipped to deal with the complex technological development of cinema. Less interested in visual perception, either its absence or presence, though his early work begins there, O'Hara's response centers around a critique of denotation that doubles as an embrace of denotation. His superabundance of reference—literally thousands of proper names—undermines the modernist's fraught relation to the word. What seemed a paradox is not one in an O'Hara poem; outshowmanship and unbridled affection for the cinema are compatible. There is no precedent for O'Hara's ability to embrace, mime, critique, and out-star new Hollywood technologies and film stars. No other American poet casts off taboos, and so dissolves the threat of technology while profiting from and laughing at its excesses. Positioned as the poet who collapses the paradox of poetry and technology, O'Hara is this book's crucial third paragon; he opens the way for new intermedia exchange and for what is possible in poetic experimentation, both in his generation and those to come.

The question that grips the American poet concerning technology can be cast numerously. Biographical evidence of the poets' hard-fought interests in sound and music suggests that the problem can be recast in terms of auditory technology.[22] By focusing specifically on the physiological sense of sight, however, I focus on the sense I take to have the most impact in the new technologies, and the one unquestionably absent in the poetic medium. For it is the sightlessness of poetry that most dramatizes the historic gap that opens between poetry and technology in the twentieth century. The shortcomings of vision that the poets stage also lead interestingly, in both creative poetics and critical thinking, to explorations of tactility and seeming materiality. Work by Elaine Scarry and Peter Schwenger[23] pushes forward this terrain of projected palpability that is, though challenging to discuss because so elusive, and dependent on the imagination, one of the speculative areas this book explores as a form of poetic critique to photorealism. Abstraction, as a response to the dominance of the eye in modernity, is balanced in the poetry of Stevens, Bishop and O'Hara, by an artistic fascination with the palpably particulate. I argue that it is the contradictory relation between the two, and the site of contact with a material that is strange to poetry—a poetically imaginary site and a technologically real site—that produces a stunning array of effects that can be called American cultural poetic critique.

WORD SIGHTINGS

CHAPTER I

Postcards to New Haven: Wallace Stevens

ROME

On January 27, 1949, Wallace Stevens wrote to his new Irish correspondent, the poet and art critic Thomas McGreevy: "Your postcard from Rome set me up. Rome is not ordinarily on the itinerary of my imagination. It is a little out of the way, covered by cypresses. It is not a place one visits frequently like Paris or Dublin."[1] McGreevy joined Stevens' growing list of "intangible and elusive friends" (*L*, 667) from whom he solicited postcards and other tangible tokens of life abroad.[2] Stevens never in his lifetime visited Rome, Paris, or Dublin, and in fact traveled out of the United States only on brief trips to Canada, Cuba, and once through the Panama Canal. Yet he cultivated an insider's knowledge of the climate, landscape, culture, and mores of foreign cities and regions. He was fascinated by such seeming irrelevancies as the noisiness of neighbors in Paris (*L*, 657), the remoteness of a skating rink on a Swiss mountaintop (*L*, 643), or the color of paint on Irish public buses (*L*, 611).

Stevens' interest in vicarious foreign living—for he wished to avoid "intellectual tourism"[3]—peaked as he approached the age of seventy, when a prominent theme of his letters became one of pleasure and commentary upon receiving postcards, pictures, books, catalogues, newspapers and local objects from abroad. This was during the late 1940s and early 1950s, the postwar decade and the last of his life, when it became most clear that Stevens would never travel to Europe. Among the dozens of requests he made during these years were for a series postcards from Madrid (*L*, 630), "native and real" figurines from Ceylon (*L*, 614) a still life painting by the French painter, Tal Coat (*L*, 637), reproductions of pictures from a Swiss villa (*L*, 645), a catalogue of exhibition paintings by Jack B. Yeats (*L*, 596), a small French volume, *Le Voyage autour de ma chambre* (*L*, 653), and copies of the Parisian newspaper, *Figaro*.[4]

Each of these items personally connected him to points abroad, stretching his imagination beyond the static regularity of his office in Hartford and his home in New Haven. But the item he most coveted was the postcard. Stevens avidly solicited what he called "tokens" of his friends' wanderings abroad,[5] writing in a letter, "I survive on postcards from Europe" (L, 797). Disappointed by a lean summer, when friends neglected to send postcards, he commented how he had "looked forward to a particularly busy summer running around all over Europe (in other people's shoes)" (L, 689).

A postcard such as McGreevy's provided the necessary and sufficient reference point for Stevens' imaginary travel. Dated November 29, 1948, to Mr. Wallace Stevens at the Hartford Accident & Indemnity Company, the black and white pictorial postcard gives a typical tourist's view of the Roman Forum, backed by a message from McGreevy about his first experience of the wind and light in Rome at that time of year. At first glance, the picture side of the postcard offers a generic view of Rome that gives little insight into the experience of living in the city. Evacuated of past or present human activity, the photograph is precisely the sort of vast, appropriative view that would invite intellectual tourism.

What draws Stevens to the Rome postcard? To borrow the terms of his poetry, the postcard gives an ordinary, plain view of things as they are: Roman columns, a hill, a few olive trees, and dark clouds overhead. Instead of being "a little out of the way, covered by cypresses," Rome is suddenly visible in its irrefutable reality. Stevens' exaggerated claim to being a visitor of Rome, simply by receiving a postcard, signals why this transparent visibility is important. The photograph, precisely by satisfying Stevens' desire to *see* Rome, covers over the technologically derived character of his sensory claim on Rome. The indexicality of the photograph invites Stevens to believe that seeing Rome is interchangeable with actually having been there. The fact that the postcard is not entirely effective, and that nobody is fooled including Stevens, is crucial to understanding this poet's stance on technology.

The sardonic edge to Stevens' accounts of actually visiting places via postcards is the key. In part his language registers an earnest personal pleasure in photographic reproduction; in part it registers a defensive stance toward visual media. Stevens' ruse is to bypass the photographic image as copy, and make a claim on its content only. If the technological medium is rendered invisible and unimportant, it has no potential for art function; the photograph poses no threat to linguistic expression at all. Stevens' verbal account of a photo image, I propose in this chapter, can be used as a tool in decrypting how his poetry works.

Stevens' ambivalence is by no means unique to himself, nor to the situation of the mid-century poet. Barthes, image-text semiotician par excellence, explains how this ambivalence works on a structural level, both in his writings on "photographic paradox," a denotative structure technology brings to the fore, and in his writings on the "reality effect," the modern literary analogue to the photo-realistic effect.[6] The viewer receives an impression of pure denotation, in Barthes' widely assimilated photographic model, even though the photograph can never be more than a copy. And this photo-denotative experience is linked, not to the feeling of *being-there*, but to the feeling of *having-been-there*. This distinction is apparent in Stevens' response to receiving a postcard in that he casts his awareness, or sense, of *having-been-there* as a literal sensory experience, despite his foreclosure from actually seeing, hearing, touching, smelling or tasting Rome. Stevens conveys to McGreevy not just the awareness, but the experience, of *having-been-there* via the postcard. He also deftly appropriates the structure of photo-realism for language by reenacting the site of denotative impasse in his account of the Rome postcard. Stevens thus harnesses the technological pretense not just to produce, rather than reproduce, reality; additionally he partakes in the particularly photographic access to nostalgic feeling in which the process of identifying through a photograph with a place or set of referents suggests an original experience more profound even than its basis in reality. Precisely those aspects of photographic reproduction that make a claim on viewers, and that place technology on top, and poetry on the bottom, of a modern hierarchy of mimesis, are ones Stevens explores here, and that he will turn to advantage in the poetry.

The representational structure of the postcard, historically, invites precisely this move, to be a virtual visitor of an actual place. A brief history of the genre shows that the postcard, more than any other form of postal correspondence, materializes the individual sender's desire to circulate the message to friends and relations of *having-been-there*.[7] And this sense is further accentuated in the particular case of the Rome postcard by the focus on ancient Roman monuments—the present remainders, as in Shelley's paradox of Ozymandias, of an absent civilization. It is worth noting that Stevens is the only party excluded from the original point of *having-been-there*. Further, he derives a certain amount of pleasure from accentuating this exterior status. By casting his "itinerary of the imagination" as an actual itinerary, Stevens visits, along with Rome, the site of denotative failure. Here is this book's first example of an American poet converting the poetry genre's lack, vis-à-vis the photographic claim to the real, into a coveted advantage: the linguistic superiority of the imaginary.

Stevens is, predictably, divided about a claim to seeing Rome when he names the city in "An Ordinary Evening in New Haven," the long poem he composed in the spring and summer of 1949. Rome is described as "after dark" in canto XXVIII, among a list of actual places that combine the "real and unreal."

> Real and unreal are two in one: New Haven
> Before and after one arrives or, say,

Bergamo on a postcard, Rome after dark,
Sweden described, Salzburg with shaded eyes
Or Paris in conversation at a café.[8]

In naming the cities from which he received postcards and photographs
that year, Bergamo, Rome and Salzburg among them, Stevens curiously
does not ask the reader to picture the cities in a visual detail comparable to
their photo-images. He defers this descriptive privilege of the poet, even
willfully excludes himself from it given the Western tradition of descrip-
tion-saturated poetry. The phrase "with shaded eyes," for example,
obscures rather than clarifies the link to the July 1949 photograph he
received of Barbara Church and Laura Sweeney in sunglasses. Stevens likewise pares down Church's postcard from Stockholm to the reflexive, unde-
scriptive phrase, "Sweden described," or reduces her lively account of a
particular conversation at a "little café near Notre Dame on the sidewalks
overlooking the Seine." By distilling the places into a stanzaic list, Stevens
generates his own serial structure.

Seriality has its own role in postcard history, as Naomi Schor explains
in her work on turn-of-the-century Paris postcards, drawing from Susan
Stewart and Jean Baudrillard, because it distinguishes the collection of
postcards from the postcard as souvenir.[9] Schor traces power structures at
play in historical uses and conceptions of the postcard as anything but
transparent, ranging from Parisian panoptic control of monuments and city
scenes, to the exposed postcard messages as invitations to encryption. The
notion of the collector is one that is especially rife with issues of appropriative power. The collector, especially one who invents his own seriality
as Stevens does, to some extent attempts to "author" the places on the
postcards by subordinating the particular interest of each card to an overarching order. For Stevens, the drive to "order," a crucially repeating word
in his work, means in this case the conversion of vicarious experiences of
each European city into the generic experience of place. Each detail
obscures or displaces the direct experience of the named place—"before
and after one arrives," "on a postcard," "after dark," "described," "with
shaded eyes," "in conversation at a café"—and suspends them within the
rhetorical order Stevens provides. For if one wanted to learn about the
actual differences between Paris and Salzburg, it would not be possible
here, because this is Stevens' rhetorical Paris, and his rhetorical Salzburg.

His effort, a difficult one indeed, is to modify not the actual cities, but
the names for the cities. This avoidance of attaching accents or particular
images to each city or country is conspicuous in "An Ordinary Evening,"
when compared with Stevens' attention to subtle details about the places
he discusses in his correspondence of the same year. The following excerpt
from an August 23, 1949 letter to Church compares the mountain landscape of Germany, as seen in a photograph, with the Pennsylvania hills of
Stevens' youth:

The mountain back of the house is much more of a mountain than anything at home, but I imagine that it gives those that live in the house the same feeling that the mountains at home give to the people who live there. The picture that you sent takes me away from the clichés of Germany. (*L*, 645)

Evident in this passage is how seriously Stevens treats his vicarious travel, and how carefully he studies a photograph in order to note shades of difference in how individual landscapes make one feel. Curiously, his emphasis here contrasts with that of "An Ordinary Evening," where the effort is to reattach places to clichés, as Bergamo to a postcard, and Paris to a café. As Stevens shifts from photograph to poem, what I believe we witness is a rejection of visual description—that easily clichéd element of poetry—through the reordering of places into discursive experiences. By describing description rather than enacting it, and by naming proper names rather than actual places, Stevens avoids a direct confrontation with the postcard picture of Rome. He collects Rome, and reorders it into the *sense* of language.

Stevens' sense of words, in both senses—the sense of the meaning of words and the perceptual sense of the words in poetry—is the central focus of this chapter, for I believe it is central to his aesthetic project. The name or word, as in the case of the place name, functions much as the object does in phenomenology. The rubrics of place and the postcard, both for Stevens and this analysis, provide indices to observing the sensation of language at work. Both the place name and the postcard set up the expectation of actual sense experience, but Stevens frustrates this expectation in order to generate the one positive sensation available to poetry: the sensation of *not* seeing, hearing, touching, tasting, or smelling the way we thought we were going to, but instead, of having the capacity for sense turned upon language.

I frame this experience of language or the word as such—and of reading as a kind of sixth sense—principally around the visual sense, and the negation of seeing in the expected way. This is not because Stevens privileges sound, though Ancu Rosu makes an important case for the workings of sound in Stevens,[10] but because vision, in the modern hierarchy of the senses, needs first to be disabled in order for language to function as all-sense substitute. Vision is merely one among all the senses, albeit the most charged and obvious one, and therefore good for the purposes of this discussion. Actual sounds also, like actual images, are subordinated to this more generalized state of sense—that is, the obscure Stevensian sense of words that tends either to attract or to repel readers, or both at once.

Here, and in the following section, "New Haven," I set up the postcard photograph as the "recto" to Stevens' "verso"; his poetry as the dark, scriptural message to the rise of photo-realism in modern life. Thus I begin with the most potent challenge to Stevens' word sense, which is the bold, still, denotative photograph. In the middle sections, which also double as

place names, "Reading" and Havana," I examine the paradox of the seeming presence, and the actual absence, of all five senses. The final section,
"Aix-en-Provence," looks at the foreclosure of actual sound, despite poetry's strongest claim on sound, in the poem, "Autumn Refrain."

The postcard as a rubric for reading Stevens' poetry requires a certain
finesse, for one side of the card makes seductive claims to photo-realism,
and the other sets up the sender as verbal witness of a place. Alan Filreis,
in an otherwise historically astute analysis of Stevens in "The Postcard
Imagination,"[11] enters the referential trap by measuring the degree of
Stevens' acknowledgement of European political realities through a comparison of poems and postcards. Doublesidedness in the postcard, according to Filreis, is an ideal view on the front, and a description of the actual
world on the back. The present study makes no assumptions as to one side
of the postcard being empirically more real, nor to Stevens' curious insis-
tences on the actual world as corresponding to reality *per se*. For Filreis,
the postcard's status as historical artifact forces the discussion down a referential track, because it assumes that Stevens has a relationship to history
that is remotely like one we know. As I understand it, Stevens' evocations
of history and the actual world are a ruse, and what he is most after is a
highly complex and sublimated poetic critique of the idea of reality *tout
court*. The project is subversive, not to say idiosyncratic, and the postcard
is just one material hinge that can allow insight into how the project not
only relies upon the negation of particulate sensation, but how that negation is proposed as its own experience.

The postcard is attractive to Stevens, as poet, because it prompts claims
upon the real that the poetry can debunk. The doublesided structure further provides a stage for the disabling of the image, but not, importantly,
for the victory of sound. Rather, the message side of the postcard is allied
with a verbal reality, which it is a mistake to ally, as Filreis does in the very
title of his book, with an actual world external to the self-reflexive encir-
cling lexicon. Given Stevens' materialist-resistant methods, it would be surprising if there was work on photo-realism and his poetry. The present
study purports to open the field first by exposing the hermeneutic trap
Stevens sets for his readers of blacking out the indexical image just where
he gives us the cue to see something. To think of Stevens as responding to
photography at such a juncture runs contrary to sense, for the reader is not
prompted to imagine photographic images. A further impediment to
explicit dialogue between poetry and visual technologies in Stevens studies
is the relatively recent precedent for interart study among poetry critics at
a representational level; most of the work has been done on a thematic level
of influence and counterinfluence.

Two of Stevens' best known critics, Helen Vendler and Harold Bloom,
argue eloquently for his intertextuality and revisioning of English and
American romanticism, while avoiding Stevens' deeply embedded engage-

ment with cultural and historical contexts—represented in synecdoche here by the "postcard"—that threaten to marginalize his aesthetic tradition. The approach of Lisa Steinman, one of the few critics to contextualize Stevens with respect to technology, makes more sense with regard to poets who adopt a less resistant stance toward referentiality such as Williams and Moore. She does speculate that Stevens' apparent silence about America and its technology could be an objection to direct comparisons between poetry and fields of more obvious utility.[12]

The ample treatments of Stevens and painting in the two decades, most notably by Charles Altieri, Bonnie Costello, and Glen MacLeod,[13] attest to the enthusiastic climate of interdisciplinary studies in Stevens criticism, within received parameters of what qualifies for comparison. Stevens' own expressed leanings confirm painting as a natural subject for comparative analysis, as does the extensive history of ekphrasis in the "sister arts."[14] The postcard, and more generally the photograph, however, intensify what comparisons with painting—especially such artists as Mondrian, Klee, and Picasso—easily obscure, because of the strong impulse to focus on similarities rather than differences between modern art and Stevens' poetry: the negative status of the indexical image in Stevens' work. During the same period in which modern painters are performing the wild experiments in abstraction that Stevens found so compelling, the picture postcard retains a high degree of indexicality—a certain gauche, commercial framing of the documentary and the picturesque.

What quickly becomes evident in reading Stevens *reading* his postcards is how strongly he rejects the ekphrastic tradition. Costello provides the sharpest commentary on the non-mimetic pose Stevens adopts vis-à-vis the visual arts. Noting how Stevens adopts the large term "art" to erase rather than account for verbal-visual differences in his essay, "The Relations Between Poetry and Painting," Costello borrows from Pater to argue that analogy significantly differs from imitation in that it invokes the condition of another art form (its representational structure and its special mode or quality of beauty) by the particular medium of one's own art. Rather than imitating visual art, or attempting to recreate its effects through language, Stevens invokes what Costello calls a "meta-analogy" between poetry and painting. Like Stevens' grandiose prose essays, however, the nature of her argument runs the risk of abstraction, and of annulling significant differences and antagonisms between the arts that might help us to read how Stevens' poetry *reads*.

To look for a postcard-image in Stevens' poetry is to look in vain, even in a case such as "The Irish Cliffs of Moher," in which Stevens meditates on a postcard he received in 1952 of the Cliffs of Moher.[15] There is no attempt in the poetry to compete with or to copy the photo-realism of the postcard. What we witness with the word "Rome" is not imitation, nor is it simple analogy; the word, in Stevens' admiringly hostile takeover of photographic denotation, fills the reader's sense by force in the denotation of the pure word.[16] According to the evidence of the written correspondence, Stevens relishes falling into the mimetic trap set up by the postcard. But the example of the Rome postcard shows how the rules change when Stevens makes the shift into writing poetry. The trap is set for the reader: the reader expects to see Rome, only to encounter a blockage of vision, and of sense in general.[17]

Generic words such as "sense" or "reality" compose much of Stevens' lexicon, prompting Bloom to comment that the word "reality" appears so frequently, and with such conflicting inflections in Stevens' poetry, that it becomes confusing, and ceases to signify anything in particular.[18] Strangely, this point can also be made of Stevens' use of proper names. "Rome" should produce a stronger effect of sound, picture and affection as an aggregate word than should a simple abstract word such as "green" or "cold," or a compounded abstract word such as "justice" or "liberty." This is to borrow Edmund Burke's two hundred and fifty year-old schema, but in a parallel context; Burke, arguing for the weakness of language to produce sensible images, writes that aggregate words operate "not by presenting any image to the mind, but by having, from use, the same effect on being mentioned that their original has when it is seen."[19] But Stevens frustrates the reader's effort to experience "Rome"—a proper name, and therefore the most concentrated instance of the aggregate word—as an actual place in the way that McGreevy sees it, or as Stevens sees it through the postcard. Instead, the proper name is granted the same weight and quality as the compounded abstract words which Stevens employs in the second half of canto XXVIII: "theory," "poetry," "life," "nothingness," "worlds."

The proper name is an obvious starting point (simple abstracts like colors and sound follow in the later section of this chapter), precisely because the proper name poses the greatest resistance to Stevens' rhetorical project. The most literal, particular, and referential words present the strongest challenge to the poet—to Stevens, and to Bishop, who we will see extend the project—because they are the ones most easily conflated with actual things. Similarly, the most indexical, vivid, photo-realist image presents a poet with the strongest challenge to compete with it, or in Stevens' case, to block it out. Eleanor Cook eloquently notes how there are a surprising number of actual names in the work, despite the curious effect in one's memory of there being not many.[20] This is because Stevens sets up the proper name to produce a black-out effect, an instant forgetfulness of the particular place or person it identifies.

The Rome postcard provides a clue to how this works. On the upper margin of the pictorial side of the card is the unusual detail of dark clouds above the Roman Forum. To the extent that the Stevens poem asks the reader to picture Rome at all, it is in the form of an anti-image, "after dark." The reader may take this as a transparent cue to imagine the actual city of Rome after the sun has gone down. But there is an additional, more revealing interpretation, prompted by the appearance of dark clouds in the photograph. The weakness of the words and lines to produce images is associated, from the opening canto of "An Ordinary Evening," with dark-ness in the face of the sun. Clouds are nature's signifiers of encroaching darkness, the obscuring of sunlight. At the upper edge of McGreevy's card, the clouds occupy the liminal position between the pictorial and scriptural sides of the postcard. To turn over the card is to cover (and thus, to black out) the picture, since the two sides of the postcard are inseparable, and cannot be seen/read simultaneously.[21] Paradoxically, McGreevy's message on the flip side of the card describes the brilliant sunlight in Rome: "A thought of you inevitable in Rome. I have never hit it in November before and am glad to have seen it in this sunlight—unbelievable at the time of year, tho' the tramontana wind makes it cold night and morning."[22] The Rome postcard gives a verbal description of sunlight on one side of the card, and a visual image of dark clouds on the other. Here, in addition to being a "perfectly reversible semiotic object" (Schor, 237), the postcard is the perfectly paradoxical token of reading seeing, and conversely, of seeing reading.

Figure 1.1. Picture side of Rome postcard. Thomas MacGreevy to Wallace Stevens, November, 29, 1948, WAS 150. This item is reproduced by permission of *The Huntington Library, San Marino, California.*

Figure 1.2. MacGreevy, message side. This item is reproduced by permission of the *Huntington Library, San Marino, California.*

    Postcard convention confirms the primacy of the image, as it dictates that the pictorial side of the postcard be examined first—often subsequently to be put on display, as Stevens often did. The scriptural side often refers back to the picture, since the writing always follows the purchase of the card, and the sender often wishes to clarify his or her exact location within the image, and/or to relay personal experiences of the depicted place. But in the Rome postcard, the discrepancy between the verbal account of the climate and its appearance in the photograph signals a contradiction, rather than simple complementarity, between the two sides. For what one actually sees is cloud cover, but what one reads is the experience of having seen sunlight. Recall in this context Stevens' comment: "Rome is not ordinarily on the itinerary of my imagination. It is a little out of the way, covered by cypresses."[23] The postcard uncovers what is usually covered in Stevens' mind by supplying a visible picture. But when Rome reappears in "An Ordinary Evening," months after his acknowledged receipt of the postcard, it is covered over once again: "Rome after dark."
    The very openness of the postcard that marked it as revolutionary in its early days also prompts, in some cases, the desire to cover it over, and to re-enclose it in an envelope.[24] Fear of exposure attaches principally to the

written side of the card, for it is there that the author is revealed, and connected to the addressee. But for Stevens, there is a deeper, metaphorical threat to the "writing" face of the card, given its inseparability from the picture face of the card. For what if the two sides of the postcard are not equal, and the word-image binary favors the picture side? The Huntington Collection of Stevens' correspondence attests to his enthusiastic interest in the postcard, especially at a late phase in life; from this it does not follow, however, that the postcard bears a simple, complementary relation to his poetry. On the contrary, the case of the Rome postcard signals how the open margin between image and word—the "two-in-one" character of the postcard—enhances a contradiction in his work.

At the lower margin of the pictorial side of the Rome postcard, in white letters, is the inscription, "*Roma—Foro Romano—Tempio di Antonino e Faustino.*" Both "forum" and "temple" derive from the sense of an open, shared space. To be visible, the proper names that identify the pictured city and monument have to be whited-in by virtue of sharing the iconic space of the card. Rather than dominant black letters against a white page, this is writing *against* the image. The postcard materializes the face-off between word and image into a token, with open margins, of the potentially subordinated status of writing in an increasingly visual age. Singled out from among Stevens' acquisitions of visual materials from abroad, including the catalogues, photographs, and extensive collection of paintings, the postcard is uniquely situated as an object of reversible binaries: word and image, absence and presence, aesthetic and commercial exchange.

NEW HAVEN

In an oeuvre extending from 1914 to 1955, Stevens' longest and most austere meditation upon the negation and linguistic recovery of the sensory imagination is the late poem, "An Ordinary Evening in New Haven." Stevens wrote the poem for the Connecticut Academy of Arts and Sciences, and read an abbreviated version of it at their meeting in November 1949. In canto XXVIII, we saw how Stevens balances his experiment with language-sense at the margin between light and dark, evening. This evening is also the leveling out of differences between place names: the balancing of particulate sensations into one generic sense. Additionally, this is an *ordinary* evening, and the etymological roots, "orderly" (*ordinarius*) and "order" (*ordo, ordin*), inform this usage of ordinary. Stevens' comment that "Rome is not *ordinarily* on the itinerary of my imagination," is significant in this context, as is the fact that the most exotic place Stevens actually visited repeatedly in his lifetime—Key West, Florida—is named in the poem title, "The Idea of Order at Key West." From the safe distance of his office and home in Connecticut, this connoisseur of foreign places, and collector of exotica, had an ordinary place in which to enjoy the disorder of sensations associated with the foreign and exotic.

In the life of a collector, Benjamin writes, there is a "dialectical tension between the poles of order and disorder."[25] This is a familiar binary of Stevens' lexicon and ars poetica, but for Stevens, the pole of disorder is a place in his imagination, rather than part of an actual itinerary. The strategies and tactical instincts Benjamin ascribes to the collector are mediated in Stevens' case, not through foreign places but through postal correspondence with contacts in foreign places. Stevens' order is mail-order, as he wrote: "I never really lived until I had a home, and my own room, say, with a package of books from Paris or London" (*L*, 301). Benjamin describes a very different relation to memories, in the essay, "Unpacking My Library," as each volume conjures up a recollected place from his past: "Memories of the cities in which I found so many things: Riga, Naples, Munich, Danzig, Moscow, Florence, Basel, Paris; memories of Rosenthal's sumptuous rooms in Munich, of the Danzig Stockturm . . . ." Benjamin's list of cities is laced with nostalgia for the particular, original sensations experienced in Riga, Naples, Moscow, and Munich. For Stevens, the American collector of postcards from European cities he has never visited, the place names Bergamo, Rome, and Salzburg sound more like just that, place names.

Stevens' ordering and evening of sensations, at the receipt of material tokens from abroad, occurs in the present tense. In this sense, he does not *arrive* in New Haven, for he is half-elsewhere, always "before and after one arrives." By evening out places into their names, rather than evoking a rich store of memories associated with cities, Stevens displaces the economy of nostalgia onto present-tense language experience. One is not homesick for a place or one's past (homesickness being the root of nostalgia), but at home in New Haven, homesick for the sensation of the absence within home-places. The feeling of something lacking circulates within language, and its referential reach toward places, people, things—"Bergamo on a postcard"—conveys rather than fills the lack.

Stevens grants a special importance to the canto immediately following canto XXVIII by placing it last in the short version of the poem.[26] Starting here, and reading in reverse, this highly complex poem is more comprehensible in its abbreviated version, as a comment upon an exotic, or extraordinary, relation to language in an ordinary place. Less a plain man in a plain town that the poem announces (canto IV, *CP*), Stevens knows himself as something of a traveler, or stranger, in his own town. The final odyssey from "the land of elm trees" (New Haven)[27] to "the land of the lemon trees" (Key West, Havana, Rome) proves to be as much a discovery of sameness as of difference.

> In the land of the lemon trees, yellow and yellow were
> Yellow-blue, yellow-green, pungent with citron-sap,
> Dangling and spangling, the mic-mac of mocking birds.

> In the land of the elm trees, wandering mariners
> Looked on big women, whose ruddy-ripe images
> Wreathed round and round the round wreath of autumn.
>
> They rolled their r's, there in the land of the citrons.
> In the land of the big mariners, the words they spoke
> Were mere brown clods, mere catching weeds of talk.
>
> When the mariners came to the land of the lemon trees,
> At last, in that blond atmosphere, bronzed hard,
> They said, "We are back once more in the land of the elm trees,
>
> But folded over, turned round." It was the same,
> Except for the adjectives, an alteration
> Of words that was a change of nature, more
>
> Than the difference that clouds make over a town.
> The countrymen were changed and each constant thing.
> Their dark-colored words had redescribed the citrons. (*CP*, 486–487)

The land of the lemon trees is yellow, blond, "pungent with citron-sap," "the mic-mac of mocking birds"—a place of sensory fullness, light, tastes, odours and song. The land of the elm trees is a place of language, where the words are "mere brown clods, mere catching weeds of talk," "dark-colored." In staging a literal arrival at the land of the lemon trees, Stevens once again generates an itinerary of the imagination. The fundamental relation between these two fictional places, as between New Haven and Rome, is one of equivalence, "evening," and interchangeability. But there is a crucial turn, or folding over, at the level of language, that alters the experience of the place. The nouns "land" and "land," and "trees" and "trees," are nominally interchangeable, but the adjectives are not. "Lemon" and "elm," nouns that function in the poem as adjectives, are the same word but turned round—as in the invertibility of the postcard. These two fictionally literal places are composed of interchangeable letters, "elm" and "lem." The difference between two places is cast as a difference of language, and in this case, of the direction in which one reads.

The doubled "yellow and yellow" that marks the internal coherence of the land of the lemon trees is changed, re-described, and read/seen differently by the outsiders as "yellow-blue, yellow-green." Initially placed as nouns, "yellow and yellow" shift to modify blue and green, and thus are altered into adjectives. This folding over, or turning round, of adjective and noun, crucially occurs over the difference between light and dark. Here the Rome postcard becomes helpful once again. For this canto fills in and complicates the phrase, "Rome after dark," from the previous canto: "It was the same, / Except for the adjectives, an alteration / Of words that was a change of nature, more / than the difference that clouds make over a town." The pun upon "change of nature" points to a further meaning beyond that of mere climate change. The liminal dark clouds—here a composite of "brown clods" and "dark-colored words"—signify the difference between seeing and reading, between seeing Rome cloudy and reading Rome sunny. This is the pictorial side of the Rome card folded over, turned round; Stevens here grants language priority over the image, giving it the capacity to change by redescription, and by the placement and mode of reading a particular word. This poem sets up words as themselves "dark-colored," with the capacity to utter dark, but not such that they darken utterly the scene. Instead, the words function to recast lemon trees as citrons, and thus to change adjectives into nouns, and English into a romance language.

The noun in Stevens is the privileged form of speech. It most closely approximates pure denotation, the name as such. The impossible task of purifying poetic language of concrete reference is increasingly compelling to Stevens in the late work. Adjectives pose the greatest challenge to the generic experience of language because they suggest subtle differences of particulate, sensory experience. Especially in the poetry after *Harmonium* (1923), and sharpened to a defining edge in the late books, Stevens attempts to strip away visual images and discrete sensations by converting adjectives into untied, free-circulating words—by turning the inevitability of modification back upon language itself. This project is announced in the opening canto of "An Ordinary Evening," in which rather than being given a plain view of a concrete scene—as of buildings, trees and clouds—we encounter the phrase, "The eye's plain version." Language, in describing transparent seeing, becomes a concrete block to seeing.

> The eye's plain version is a thing apart,
> A few words, an and yet, and yet, and yet—
>
> As part of the never-ending meditation,
> Part of the question that is a giant himself:
> Of what is this house composed if not the sun,
>
> These houses, these difficult objects, dilapidate
> Appearances of what appearances,
> Words, lines, not meanings, not communications,
>
> Dark things without a double, after all,
> Unless a second giant kills the first— (*CP*, 465)

The doubling and tripling of words in this canto creates a slippage that acts like a sublime, alerting us to the disfiguration at the heart of figuration.

"And yet and yet and yet," or "appearances of what appearances" leave the reader with nothing concrete to grasp onto, save the noun-sense produced by the repetition of words. Words and lines are named, and are attached to "not meanings" and "not communications." Writing is coded as a dark, concrete thing without a double. This is the scriptural side of the postcard impossibly detached from its pictorial side.

As if performing a surgery on the act of writing itself, Stevens takes us into a reflection upon the rhetorical structures and components of poetry, moving in cantos VI through XII of the long version of the poem through a dissection of meaning at the level of the letter, the sound, the syllable, the word, the phrase, and the poem.

> Reality is the beginning not the end,
> Naked Alpha, not the hierophant Omega,
> Of dense investiture, with luminous vassals.
>
> It is the infant A standing on infant legs,
> Not twisted, stooping, polymathic Z,
> He that kneels always on the edge of space
>
> In the pallid perceptions of its distances.
> Alpha fears men or else Omega's men
> Or else his prolongations of the human. (*CP*, 469)

The effect of beginning with a word (alpha) to describe a letter is that of creating a world composed entirely of internal reference and ordering. "Alpha" does not signify an image or thing outside the poem, but refers reflexively to its own verbal "reality." This reality begins literally in the material of the letter: the reader sees not the image of infant legs, but the anthropomorphizing of the literal stems of the letter "A" on the page. Reality as such begins in the naked letter, and is inseparable from the acts of writing and reading. Imagery is a disposable by-product of language, and not integral to its meaning, or to the reader's experience. To move further into the alphabet from the infant letter "A" is to enter into a land of hieroglyphs, in which the visibly legible shapes of letters take on the dimensions of corporeal beings. The expression that "Alpha fears men or else Omega's men" speaks to the threat of external reference. When the anthropomorphic characters of the alphabet mature into men—"the hierophant Omega" and "the polymathic Z"—they are banished because of their learning and sophistication into bare letters.

The paradox of written poetry, that one does not hear or see one's own creations, means that the poet is forced to imagine sound, and to utter images. This is evident in the line, "the cry that contains its converse in itself." When Stevens says "cry," the immediacy of the statement blocks out, or stands in place of the silence, or lack of sound: he is not re-creating a sound, nor is he asking the reader to create a sound in her own ear, but what is signified is "sound." Here Stevens proposes a uniquely poetic experience of the word, "sound," not as a memory or association with sensation, but as its own positive sensation. At the same time, Stevens calls attention to the sound, syllables, and letters of the words he uses. Consider the double-meaning of the word "converse," which means both "the opposite to" and "the act of conversing with." Stevens brings together noun and verb forms in a single paradoxical turn of phrase. The syllable "verse" adds to the paradox, literally meaning "to turn" (from the Latin *vertere*), in addition to being a synonym for poetry. In a single gesture, the words turn away from and turn toward the poem, as in the turning of "The Domination of Black," and the turning back and forth of the two-sided postcard.

If nothing else, the poem at least refers back to itself. Yet what is it that compels Stevens to seek out this absence within places, and within actual sensations, when language, in its metaphoric resilience, cannot lose its associations with place and sense? The desire to find an irreducible non-metaphoric core to poetry, one that is illogically pre-verbal, is balanced by a coexistent and coequal desire: this I propose is Stevens' enactment, in parallel with Stein's, of how poetic language re-emerges with its tropes and sensory virtuality intact. By playing out this double desire, Stevens takes a brazen American approach toward reassuring himself as to the indestructibility of poetry. Further, he underscores that the capacity to reference the world "out there"—such as lies in the technical perfection of the photograph—is not the scale by which art is measured. Stevens' most radical philosophical proposition, and the one that is hardest to reconcile with his status as family man and insurance agent, is that denotative factuality is not the scale by which experience is measured either.

The following passage from "An Ordinary Evening" advances Stevens' interest from the "letter" and the "syllable" to the "word" and the "poem," extending further his paradox of finding a pure, nonphenomenal reality of language.

> We keep coming back and coming back
> To the real: to the hotel instead of the hymns
> That fall upon it out of the wind. We seek
>
> The poem of pure reality, untouched
> By trope or deviation, straight to the word,
> Straight to the transfixing object, to the object
>
> At the exactest point at which it is itself,
> Transfixing by being purely what it is,
> A view of New Haven, say, through the certain eye

> The eye made clear of uncertainty, with the sight
> Of simple seeing, without reflection. (*CP*, 471)

The poet stands behind his poem only distantly, as if the mere sound of the words "reality," "poem," "word," or "object," is enough to transfix reality, and to block out or so converge upon the point of reference as to render it obsolete. The poem attempts to strip itself of "trope or deviation," and therein achieve a reality of sounds and words. Rhetoric needs to be technically perfected: acute, objective, with the capacity not merely to resemble, but to produce and even to replace reality. Precisely the impossibility of evading the metaphoric character of language, however, keeps Stevens' artistry from boring his readers and himself. If he can keep casting home as a hotel, as we will see him do in "Arrival at the Waldorf," then the static regularity and familiar sensory impressions of the one real place he keeps coming back to, New Haven, are sensed anew.

Note that the lines "straight to the word, / Straight to the transfixing object, to the object," generate a verbal and visual parallel between "word" and "object" such that the two are virtually interchangeable with respect to the things that they signify. Yet "word" and "object" signify different things, however generically or vaguely they are named. Stevens' desire to get past this difference, and to extend the parallel or resemblance into some third thing, emerges in his trope of chiasmus: the crossing of the straight stems of the letter "x" (in "exactest" and twice in "transfixing"), and the repetition and reordering of the words "transfixing object" and "object // . . . Transfixing." In the verbal image of the "X," Stevens achieves an "exactest point" of intersection in which such straight lines as between "poem" and "word," and "poem" and "object," cross, and superimpose differences upon a point that is located nowhere but in the poem itself (although in the last section, I examine how "X" is informed by his relation to the place, "Aix"). It is appropriate that "trope" and "deviation," both of which literally derive from "to turn," are what impede the desire for a straight, fixed point; the unavoidability of the tropes and turns of poetic form is precisely what impedes an arrival at "the poem of pure reality." The knowledge that this point, or place, does not exist, is crucial to Stevens' ars poetica.

The letter "X" figures at the end of Stevens' poem, "The Motive for Metaphor," as that which cannot be refused or transformed. It is what opposes the shadowy metaphorics of the poet who shrinks from hard speech, longing for "the obscure moon lighting an obscure world / Of things that would never be quite expressed." The close of "An Ordinary Evening," in its long version, is marked by an attention to obscure sounds and details, ambiguous and partial sensations, and the "little reds / Not often realized" (with a pun on "little reads") that are subtly present within the more certain, hard presence of experience. One ending generates the "hard sound" and "sharp flash" with all the violence of the camera shutter; the other finds the silences within sound, the unseen colors within color, and the subtle words within speech. To preserve and to find the latter in the cultural and historical moment in which he finds himself, Stevens seeks out the violent negation of the "X" and the tropic renewal that it makes possible.

READING

> For the poet's image is a spoken image; it is not an image that our eyes see. One feature of the spoken image is sufficient for us to read the poem as the echo of a vanished past.
>
> —Gaston Bachelard [28]

Stevens was born and raised in Reading, Pennsylvania in 1879, where he attended Reading Boys' School. Stevens developed a strong interest in genealogy in the 1940s, and wrote over four hundred letters to gather information about his ancestry. His letters are addressed mostly to professionals, but some are to relatives and contacts in Reading, including one to John Zimmerman Harner, dated July 23, 1945. Harner was collecting funds for the restoration of the Amityville Cemetery where some of Stevens' ancestors were buried. Stevens acknowledged his receipt of postcards of the Pennsylvania town from Harner:

> It is curious that these postcards should so soon have become a part of antiquity, or at least of the antiquated. The one of the Mansion House is particularly interesting to me. Years after my parents had died, and when I had no place to go in Reading except to the Mansion House, I went there one night and was given a room at the foot of an air shaft. . . . There I was, sentimentalizing over the fact that I was at home again, full of the milk and honey of such a state of mind, dumped into a hole in the wall with a couple of cigarette butts for company. This made me feel a certain satisfaction when the Mansion House was finally demolished. (*L*, 509)

The postcard of the Mansion House pictures a place no longer still standing, where Stevens had spent a night, ghostlike, in the displacement of no longer having a home in Reading. Over thirty years after his parents' deaths, having come of age simultaneously with the birth of the American picture postcard, Stevens comments on how soon things become part of antiquity; the postcard, once at the cutting edge of modern communication, had become the material marker of temporal loss, the passage of his relatives, and of his birthplace. Here Stevens meditates on the structure of absence-presence within the picture postcard. Not simply a representation of Reading, but a fragment of a past life there, the postcard is a "part of antiquity." Or, as Stevens emends the phrase, the postcard is "at least of the antiquated." The Reading postcard is the reverse of the Rome postcard, for it depicts a site where he has actually been, now demolished, instead of an existing site he has never seen. As such, the picture is less a window into Reading than its ghostly remainder.

With the aging of the postcard comes its alternate object status, not as a commodity—a paid, stamped exchange between sender and recipient—but as a materialized remnant of something now gone. The postcard shifts from being a reproduction of the original Mansion House to being its substitute. Reading, the town, is now a floating signifier, concrete, but without context, without a home or spatial referent, save in Stevens' mind.[29] Reading, the act, is allegorized as a detached, floating, concrete person in an audience of ghostly listeners in Stevens' poem, "Large Red Man Reading." Like relatives who have passed away, but are still present in the poet's mind, these ghosts come back with a longing for materiality, to be part of the world of reference. But in bringing them back into the presence of the poem, the poet becomes ghostly, is converted from a noun into an adjective, from Reader into Reading.

Reading, not as a place but as an act, is the ghost of reference in "Large Red Man Reading" (1948). The poem, appearing along with "An Ordinary Evening" in the *Auroras of Autumn*, is a meditation on the act of reading and its phantasmatic qualities. The challenge to seeing the figure described in the poem's title in the broadest terms of size, color, shape, and activity is that this man is read by us, and not seen, as large and red and reading. This is a "read man" whose virtual giantness ensures a space in our imaginations for considering, not the specific contours of his figure, but the impasse across which reading reaches the senses. That as readers we are foreclosed from seeing reading, and from employing any of our senses except in a virtual fashion, renders us ghostly, decorporealized figures who return to poetic language with a longing for embodiment.

The reader's desire for sound is embedded in the poem through the recurrence of aural and visual variants of "ear." The visual rhymes in the first line are themselves soundless: "There were ghosts that returned to earth to hear his phrases." To hear this line aloud is to lose the subtlety of its visible patterns; to read it silently is to lose the actual sound of words in the ear. The word "aloud" in the caesura between the reader ("As he sat there reading") and the book ("the great blue tabulae") enhances the effect of virtual-actual crossing. A silent reader who projects a real sound into the fictive space of the poem may imagine, but not hear, the presence of sound. A vocal reader, who reads "aloud" aloud, hears the echo effect of a virtual act of reading embedded within a real one.

The complex oscillation between actual and virtual sensation happens at the level of image as well as of sound. The challenge of imagining a giant reader, the ghostly listeners, and "great blue tabulae" is that these figures bear only a tenuous relation to the corporeal: their size and scope are disproportionate to our capacity to see and hear them. Such descriptive modifiers as "blue" or "large" solicit the desire to see, yet give no contextual assurance that something is really there. If the vivacity of imaginary objects is enhanced, as Elaine Scarry has suggested, by authorial instructions to perceive a context or "vertical floor" to our projected images, then part of what seems to be at issue in Stevens' poem is the sensation of the floor having dropped out.[30] Somewhere in a verbal sublime between the "earth" and the "wilderness of stars," we are nowhere: the plurality and vastness is too encompassing for the reader to extend, without risk, a dimension of corporeality to the depicted scene. Stevens disarms the reader of the quality of "givenness" that Scarry argues is crucial to perceptual mimesis.

Severed from a field of tangible reference, we acquire something of the ghostly suspension of "they" who return to the poem's scene of reading. The suspension of images such as "the great blue tabulae" in a field without gravity or corporeal dimension exposes the reader to the element of volition and coercion in image-making. Between reading and imagining, we realize our own sensory lack as readers, and "sense" our desire to enter into the poem's illusion. Susan Stewart links the desire for absolute presence in the face of the gap between signifier and signified to a theory of nostalgia. Language perpetuates nostalgia, she writes, where it would close the gap between lived and mediated experience: "When language attempts to describe the concrete, it is caught in an infinitely self-effacing gesture of inadequacy, a gesture which speaks to the gaps between our modes of cognition—those gaps between the sensual, the visual, and the linguistic."[31] To sense the giantness of the gap, and the ghostliness of sounds, is to be exposed to an insatiable perpetuation of the desire for corporeality.

Though the poem nowhere says it, Stevens wrestles in "Large Red Man Reading," with an immediate postwar context in which the technologically informed slippage between red and read, and within his personal biography, between Reading, P.A. and the act of reading, becomes an acute locus for emotions about loss and the reclaiming of sensation within poetry alone. The sensation of reading is personified in ghostly terms. In some sense, the poem seems to ask, could reading itself be dead? And how does he imagine his own readers, as grasping at something, a fiction he has put forth, that has no other grounding, no physicality? As Stevens ages, his style does not swerve from the project to strip language of its ties with corporeal sensations. It grows more intense and more spare, making *Harmonium* seem a raucous sensory parade by contrast. But if his style is part of a continuum, as it evolves by virtue of emphatic repetition, might it not—in imaginative, not empirical, terms—be slowly decorporealizing the poet? Usually the opposite assumption applies to an accomplished poet, that the accumulation of books concretizes the identity past the lived life.

For Stevens, the contest between the sensual and linguistic components of a word is one that he engages in each poem, and that predictably, since the contest is irresolvable, the next poem needs to take up as well. In "Large Red Man Reading," his use of the word "red" brings in conflict senses of desire and loss in the face of the inadequacy of language to satisfy both the senses and the intellect at once. The word becomes something like a substitute for our nostalgia, a rendering present of impossibility, and a word-sense of the gap that separates our knowledge from corporeal experience. Stewart describes what happens in the attempt to read the content of reading:

> What disappears in writing is the body and what the body knows—the visual, tactile, and aural knowledge of lived experience. Thus, whenever we speak of the content of reading, we see at work a doubling which undermines the authority of both the reading situation and the situation or locus of depiction: the reader is not in either world, but rather moves between them, and thereby moves between varieties of partial and transcendent vision. (Stewart, 44)

The ghostly irresolution is not unique to Stevens' poetry, but hovers about a first generation of modernist writers that accentuates the structure Stewart describes in order to achieve concentrated states of genre reflexivity. Stevens, extending this project as far as possible, tries to intensify rather than diminish the felt experience of the shift between the scene of reading and the written scene. He collapses the locus of depiction with that of reading, such that we arrive at the chiasmic equation in which the reading of content = the content of reading. The effect of bringing together the abstract reading act (the act of reading a book in fact being one of the more corporeal features of the genre) with the seemingly concrete content of the poem, is that our nostalgic awareness of an unbridgeable gap between the two is paradoxically enhanced even as the very distinctions are breaking down.

The sense of reading in "Large Red Man Reading" is produced through an evacuation of descriptive context. Since description is what separates and bridges the site of reading and the site of depiction, the syntactic isolation and decontextualization of imaginary objects upsets the illusion of mimetic balance. This happens in the minimal gestures toward context in the second stanza, as in the first: "There were those that returned to hear him read from the poem of life, / Of the pans above the stove, the pots on the table, the tulips among them." With its strange gravity and suspension of tactile objects, this is a profound, if desolate, writing of a non-memorial sense of concretion and presence.

The repetition of "there were" from the first stanza, rather than generating spatial or temporal clarification, doubles the uncertainty as to space and time. Stevens' choice of "those that" in place of "those who" has the effect of dehumanizing these ambiguous figures, and of rendering their very presence an absence in the reader's attempt to make them imaginatively concrete. Not knowing from whence they come, we know first that they have "returned to earth to hear," and now that they have "returned to hear." The ambiguity of the "here" to which they return is that it seems to be more a way of listening than a place, just as the "returned" speaks to the turning between stanzas as much as to the mimetic movement of the figures in the poem.

The poem's gestures toward descriptive placement, spatial context, and relationality resist imaginative resolution, such that the objects of the poem remain suspended in virtuality. The vividness of "pans above the stove" derives not from the image of a singular or original set of pans, but from our own desire to see objects in the face of the obstacles Steven sets.[32] As readers, we are exposed to our absurd capacity to imagine that we are seeing anything, anywhere, by simple relational cues ("above," "on," "among") and a few isolated signifiers ("pans," "pots," "tulips"). The vertical floor from which we spring is our own volition, as in "An Ordinary Evening," where canto XXVIII begins: "reality exists / In the mind: the tin plate, the loaf of bread on it, / The long-bladed knife . . . ."

Stevens does not grant the "pans" and the "poem" the illusion of givenness that in most literary contexts, they would have. As a result, they seem to exist only in the conscious interplay between the reader and the poem, which is of course, always the case, only we do not usually focus on this fact. But Stevens does something additional, or rather something that happens by virtue of the advertised evacuation of sensory content: the reader remarkably experiences the sensation of vivid perception nonetheless, such that the "pans" and "pots" alliteratively pop out from their non-contexts. Word-objects are felt to be suspended and arranged in imaginary space, as accentuated by the reversal of the accustomed order, "pots and pans." Part of the paradox is that the projected space for sensory forms does not need to be occupied for the reader to experience it as sense. The significant aspect of Stevens' imaginary space is the feeling of lack—and the tangible presence of a void—that predicates the projected reality of objects. Suspended in this impasse, there is a certain liberation of the senses, in which sight and touch and sound are virtually concentrated to vivify even their own absence. The superimposed presence of "pans" or "pots" therefore takes on a vivid materiality effect, as the reader is predisposed toward sensation even where there is nothing to feel.

An interchangeability of what can enter into this projected sensory space opens up, such that the word "poem" might be as vividly experienced as "pots." Once released from the one-way street of referentiality, the reader is freed to experience the back and forth, to and fro, between the concrete and the imaginary. In alienating words from their concrete associations, and by suspending objects outside of the descriptive contexts that stabilize the mimetic process, Stevens multiplies the potential for word play, from paradoxes, puns, riddles, juxtapositions, to ambiguities of time and space. The possibility for the interplay and slippage of signifiers expands when words bear a distant relation (both literal and figurative) to sense. Aural and verbal accidents are there for the making, such that in the poem's second stanza, it might as well be the "poem" or the "poets" on the table, and the reader's "two-lips" among them, where the flowers should be.[33]

Stevens' word play activates the reader in the frustrated attempt to signify—at once pleasurable and nostalgic—and in so doing, produces word-objects akin to the nouns of *Tender Buttons*. The reader is prompted to feel, not nonsense, but the sense of non-space as having tangible outlines.[34] The condition for unreal objects is that they be felt as the more real, and the mark of the real is the degree of *felt* relation to a scene, regardless of visibility or coherence. Thus the emphasis in "Large Red Man Reading" on the entrance into that which feels more real, "to step barefoot into reality," is to enter imaginatively into the letters and syllables of prosody. The ghostly presences return, not to an actual reality of kitchen pots and thorn bushes, but to the virtual site of reading, and to the feeling of its "outlines of being."

The third stanza of the poem is the most explicitly phenomenological, in which ghostly listeners "run fingers over leaves / And against the most coiled thorn." The act of reading is suspended in the past conditional tense; if reading had its own grammatical "sense," it would be the conditional, whereby everything that is felt or experienced is imaginatively projected. Stevens' use of the conditional along with the past tense compounds the implausibility that we as readers project a vividness of virtual corporeality. Such obstacles to reading are for Stevens the necessary enactment of the disassociated sensibility; the incoherence of images opens the gap across which feeling can be reattached. Yet what is enacted primarily through syntax and poetic tropes in "An Ordinary Evening" is readable in "Large Red Man Reading" through a relative continuity of tense and narrative; the gap that makes reassociation possible in this poem is tenuously explored at the level of figuration.

There is a subtle shift in the fourth stanza from a scene of depiction, however ambivalently suspended, to the present tense of the reader's self-reflexive reading of "*Poesis, poesis.*" Momentarily the awareness of the characters in the poem—giant and ghostly—modulates into the awareness of ourselves reading the words. Reading here is indeed transpersonal,[35] and further, transdimensional; the pun on "characters" acts as the hinge across which we as readers shift between literal and personified characters—like the alphabetic characters of "An Ordinary Evening." We read the ghosts and giant, and see ourselves in these personae. But we also read the words, pause at their repetition, and sense our own outlines of being in the letters, without any further content or meaning beyond. The reader's desires are momentarily housed—suspended in the repetition—when poetic process is nothing more than the sensation of itself.

The odd placement of modifiers in the phrase that follows—"the literal characters, the vatic lines"—is a cue that Stevens would suspend the reader at this site of impasse. "Vatic," derived from 'to see,' meaning prophetic or oracular, contrasts with the Mallarméan lines, the "words, lines, not meanings, not communications, / Dark things without a double" of "An

Ordinary Evening." If the "vatic" lines are to be prophetic, the crossroads of adjective/noun pairings generates a taut connection between the process of seeing and the process of reading/writing, such that even a rearrangement of modifiers to "the vatic characters, the literal lines" would loosen the mimesis-resistant syntax: we might see prophetic personae, and read material letters, rather than remain suspended between poles in a state of "representativeness."

Paradoxically, it is the monotony—the near mechanization—of the verbal construction of obects as separate from desire that enables Vendler to claim desire as Stevens' great subject. She writes of how he mercilessly renews desire such that "each moment of reflection . . . is a rebirth of the impulse toward fulfillment" (Vendler, *Desire*, 30). This is the nearly despairing humanism that Vendler would defend against critics who disparage Stevens as remote and distant. And indeed, part of Stevens' project is to reattach words to *feeling*, wherever they bear too indexical a relation to things:

> Which in those ears and in those thin, those spended hearts,
> Took on color, took on shape and the size of things as they are
> And spoke the feeling for them, which was what they had lacked.
>
> (*CP*, 13–15)

Located in the ghostliness of reading is the recovery of the sense of "color," "shape" and "size," the ancestral return of relation to Reading.

The theme of reading is traceable through a cluster of Stevens' poems, notably "The Reader," "The House was Quiet and the World was Calm," and "Phosphor Reading by his Own Light." The latter addresses the sensuous evacuation of the page: "The page is blank or a frame without a glass / Or a glass that is empty when he looks." A kind of photographic imprinting takes place whereby the book acts as the blank negative that receives, not the world reflected, but a deepening of the "greenness" that falls through the reader's act of looking. The reader's expectation and desire in the face of the negative of the page (its non-reflectiveness) is what enables the elemental recombining with primitive speech and writing. The suffusion of the "greenness" of night, through the reader and into the book, allows visual sensation and feeling to enter into the act of reading: "The greenness of night lies on the page and goes / Down deeply in the empty glass . . . // The green falls on you as you look, / Falls on and makes and gives, even a speech." The vital component of reading is not the words on the page, but the commerce between the elemental world, the reader, and the book. The non-naturalistic element of visuality that we experience in "greenness" is linked for Stevens to the negation of one form of vision in order to corporealize the reader's desire and imaginative agency in another.

"A Postcard from a Volcano," written in 1933 when Stevens received a postcard picture of a volcano from a friend in Honduras, echoes the sentiments of "Large Red Man Reading": "with our bones / We left much more, left what still is / The look of things, left what we felt / At what we saw." Curiously, "Esthétique du Mal," set next to Mount Vesuvius, contains a more explicit scene of writing from a volcano. The recognizable subject of "A Postcard from a Volcano," composed the year Stevens bought his house in New Haven, is the empty Mansion House of Reading, Pennsylvania. The poet seizes the occasion of the poem as "postcard" to render himself ghostly in advance, and to imagine a "shuttered mansion-house," emptied of content, as the remnant of his own poetic presence. In an odd, self-reflexive turn on the mode of apostrophe, Stevens imagines what children playing around the house, picking up "our bones," will say. The crucial component of his legacy is not material, but as in "Large Red Man Reading," the *feeling* of what we saw; the children "least will guess that with our bones / We left much more, left what still is / The look of things, left what we felt / At what we saw" (*CP*, 159). By substituting "Postcard" for "Poem" in the poem's title, Stevens evokes the structure of absence within presence that so quickly turns the postcard into a part of antiquity. But he evokes the structure in order to reverse it, such that poetry generates, not a picture presence—the pictorial side of the card—but the anonymous (no longer recognizable) sender's side of the card, the message: what we felt at what we saw.

HAVANA

The alter-city to Stevens' familiar New Haven is Havana, that sensuous, exotic, Latin capital of Cuba, which the austere, Northern, businessman poet first visited by ferry from Key West in February 1923. Like all the tropical cities of his travels, imaginary or actual, Havana is linked in his poetry to rich sensory experience: colors, odours, flavors, flowers and festival music, ocean surfaces, bird song, and celebration. Stevens wrote a lengthy letter to Elsie on February 4, 1923, detailing his experiences in Havana, and included descriptions of Cuban cigars, a man crying "Hot Peanuts!" a lamp-lighter on the Prado, dresses in shades of pink and orange, Sunday afternoon's procession of pedestrians and automobiles, a man on horse-back dressed in white, and a lunch of "orangeade, Cuban lobster, banana bread, cocoanut milk ice cream, and a pot of Cuban coffee" (*L*, 234–6). Stevens loved to indulge his appetite for food, as the nickname "giant" suggests (see "Large Red Man Reading"). At this stage in his life, Stevens also indulged his desire for actual travel, often alone. He added in the letter to Elsie, "Of course, I feel rather sinful about running over here to Havana. But . . . I enjoy nothing more than seeing new places and this one is new and strange from top to bottom." As Stevens aged, we recall, his desire to see new places became increasingly displaced onto his vicarious travel. His daughter, Holly Stevens, explains in her memoir, "Holidays in Reality," that Stevens felt uncomfortable with sleeping away from home toward the end of his life.[36]

By 1944, when the young Cuban, José Rodríguez-Feo, editor of a little magazine *Origenes*, and recent Harvard graduate, contacted him for permission to publish some of his poems in Spanish translation, Stevens was ready for a long, vicarious journey back to Cuba. The correspondence with the young Cuban lasted until the end of his life.[37] In July 1949, Stevens wrote to José (one of the few he addressed by first name) in Havana, "Your postcard from Varadero Beach is on my dresser at home, where the surf of it rolls day and night making mild Cuban sounds" (*L*, 643). Stevens' enthusiasm for his Cuban contact, as Richardson suggests, likely derived from the fact that Havana was one of the few places conjured in his imagination that had a counterpart in his actual experience (Richardson, 243).

In the first postcard to Elsie from Havana on February 3, 1923, Stevens wrote on the back of a picture of downtown Havana, "The place is foreign beyond belief."[38] A second postcard from the same trip pictures the Hotel Sevilla in Havana, and reads in its entirety: "Sunday. This is a picture of my hotel. The building at the right hand side is the Clerk's Club. On the other side of the square is the Presidential Palace. W.S." It is hard to imagine a more point-blank message, as Stevens names and indexically points to each building in the photograph. We recall from the letter that Sunday was the day of the procession, full of new sights and sounds and sense experiences. The contrast between the letter, full of details and impressions, and the postcard, an extremely pared down version of sight-seeing, is significant. It prefigures the discrepancy noted earlier between Stevens' pleasure at receiving postcards in his letters, and his subsequent obscuring of the postcard pictures in his poetry.

The postcard evidently prompts a particular kind of discourse in Stevens—one in which the deictic is prominent. For the Havana postcard materializes the paradox of presence-absence: it presents a photograph of a place that is absent, and a message from someone who is absent. It is the two-faced link between Havana and New Haven that is, on the one hand, a fragment of the place, and on the other, its empty copy. As names, Havana and Haven are essentially exchangeable, for one can be read in the other, just as the "land of the lemon trees" can be read in the "land of the elm trees." And Stevens names recognizable, secure points of reference: the hotel, the square, the club, the palace. But the feeling of sensory plenitude that Stevens so meaningfully attaches to Havana, and to tropical places in general, is evacuated in the process of naming "this."

Stevens addresses this evacuation of the "perfect plenitude" of Havana neither in a letter nor a postcard, but in the poem, "Academic Discourse at Havana." First published as "Discourse in a Cantina at Havana" in November 1923,[39] Stevens' four-part poem opens with the sensuous discourse shared by the Havana letter. From the canaries, afternoon orchestras, and balloons—a near match to how "Sunday Morning" opens—Stevens vacillates to a different discourse, that of the metropoles and ivory towers of the Northern climates.

> Canaries in the morning, orchestras
> In the afternoon, balloons at night. That is
> A difference, at least, from nightingales,
> Jehovah and the great sea-worm. The air
> Is not so elemental nor the earth
> So near.
> But the sustenance of the wilderness
> Does not sustain us in the metropoles. (*CP*, 142)

Nightingales are opposed to canaries, as the metropoles are to the tropical. New England (*England*) and Havana are not complementary, but contradictory, in their two very different versions of heaven. Stevens' reported pleasure in the letter to Elsie at a man crying "Hot Peanuts!" is converted in the poem to the vituperative "a peanut parody / For peanut people," and the man on horse-back to "The thickest man on thickest stallion-back." Stevens bitterly observes how Havana and its circus of the senses are passed over by the politic man who ordains "Imagination as the fateful sin." But Stevens, too, is foreclosed, and this deepens the bitterness; not from imaginative access to the senses, but from the actual sensuous life Havana perfects. He is the poet on the hotel balcony whose "dark, pacific words" share more in common with the parent colonizers than with the wild, tropical city of casinos and cantinas that Havana epitomized in the 1920s.

Stevens' second and last trip to Havana came in November of the same year, 1923, just after the publication of *Harmonium*, as he traveled with Elsie on the boat, *Kroonland*. "Sea Surface Full of Clouds" (1924) shows Stevens converting sensory foreclosure into an asset. The paradox of presence-absence, ever more structurally exposed as his art matures, is here least evident as Stevens bathes the reader in sensory effects. Much celebrated as a "pure poem," each of the five cantos begins "In that November off Tehuantepec," repeating and recirculating nouns, but changing the adjectives with apparent whimsy. Colors and food—the favorite, repeated elements of the poem—are brought back in ever less visible and edible forms: "rosy chocolate," "chop-house chocolate," "porcelain chocolate," "musky chocolate," "Chinese chocolate." This movement, a poetry of swimming in place, conveys the pleasure in the difference that adjectives make, not between kinds of chocolate, but in the sense of words. This is a savoring and sensing of language itself. The sensory associations produced by the word "chocolate" are severed from any spatial, phenomenal referent, and allowed merely to recirculate in a kind of linguistic indulgence.

Color is especially attractive to Stevens because it is so easily abstracted from physical referents, while retaining its association with primary sensation. To name a color such as "green" is to have it both ways; like "Rome," it gives us the thing it forecloses us from, but not just at the level of a dark word. "Green" is a glowing, vibrant, springlike word that needs no reattachment to the object-world for a reader to experience its sensory effect. Little matter, then, that Stevens' progression through seven modifications of green in "Sea Surface" yields no vivid imagery of particular shades of green: "paradisial green," "swimming green," "sham-like green," "uncertain green," "too-fluent green," "thinking green," "motley green." The naming of blunt colors, as opposed to partial, evanescent shades, seems to have the effect of removing the colors from particular objects, and of producing a pure, abstract shock of color.

Stevens' penchant for solid, primary colors such as red and blue, over subtler hues like lime or olive, prompts one critic to speculate that "perhaps color enters into his reality-metaphor equation, because strong, pure, primary colors seemed most actual to him."[40] As strange as this idea is, it underscores the physiological connection between colors and the feelings they produce: one feels blue. Michael Taussig proposes that to emphasize the nonvisual—as in the example, "you feel redness"—is to register the bodily impact of imaging.[41] A hybrid of non-visual and visual words, like "thinking green," allows Stevens to subordinate the visual aspect of color, and to enhance the sensation of the word "green" as part of a generic rather than optical sense. The phrase, "thinking green," lacking in any actual sensory content of its own, is converted into the direct object of experience. The reader feels neither the structure of remembering, nor of projecting, but the primary, immediate sensation of language itself, in the present tense of reading. For it is the reader who blends the primary colors of Stevens' primitive palette in "Large Red Man Reading." The relation between reader + poem enables the equation: "Red Man" + "blue tabulae" = "purple tabulae." Since red often signals primitive energy in Stevens, and blue the imagination, the reader generates a third sensation between man and book: purple.

My purpose in treating poems from Stevens' early and mid-career books, *Harmonium* ("Sea Surface Full of Clouds"), *Ideas of Order* ("Academic Discourse at Havana"), and especially *Parts of a World* ("Arrival at the Waldorf," "Study of Two Pears," "Arcades of Philadelphia the Past," and "Poem Written at Morning,") in this section, "Havana," is to examine a more explicitly and thematically sensuous phase of his oeuvre in the context of Stevens' later, ghostlier, noun-sense phase. Havana, Cuba is the pivot point between Stevens' visits to the actual land of the senses in the early 1920s, and the ever more remote revisiting of sensation from his home in New Haven in the late 1940s. "Arrival at the Waldorf" begins with "home" and ends with

"Guatemala," and in the process shifts from a transparently actual place to an arrival at an indexical place name. Thus, the poem's most vivid, and oft-quoted line, "After that alien, point-blank, green and actual Guatemala," contains the deictic "that," substituting the name for the exotic country it no longer needs.

> You touch the hotel the way you touch moonlight
> Or sunlight and you hum and the orchestra
> Hums and you say "The world in a verse,
>
> A generation sealed, men remoter than mountains,
> Women invisible in music and motion and color,"
> After that alien, point-blank, green and actual Guatemala. (*CP*, 241)

Back in his imaginary element, and away from the Havana postcard's actual, "This is a picture of my hotel," Stevens conveys a fuller, happier, and more relaxed discourse. On the page, he can generate an amorous effect of the foreign and the actual that he conveys so blandly on the postcard back. And perhaps this is because photographic realism's claim on the visible shuts down his access to the invisible. In New Haven ("Before and after one arrives") he can metaphorically "touch the hotel," where in the Havana postcard, the hotel is too visible to be touched.

Actually to arrive, and to be visibly there, is deemed a lesser experience than to be "invisible in music and motion and color." Stevens wrote to Ronald Lane Latimer in 1935:

> I am very much afraid that what you like in my poetry is just the sort of thing that you ought not to like: say, its music or color. If that is true, then an appropriate experiment would be to write poetry without music and without color. But so many of these experiments come to nothing (*L*, 297).

Of course Stevens increasingly makes this experiment, but it is worth noting his recognition of the necessary partiality of sensory foreclosure. Color cannot be entirely blocked out or negated, which is part of its great attraction for Stevens. To name color is to combine, in the poet's terms, the real and unreal as two in one. In "The Study of Two Pears," the reader encounters not a poem without colors, but an amalgam of named and negated colors. The composing of imaginary pears (a "pair" of "pears") while seeing actual pears—"touched red," with "bits of blue," and "various yellows"—produces new, partially read (red) colors: "Citrons, oranges and greens / Flowering over the skin." Here the readerly space between the real and the imaginary is one of double superimposition; the reader sees and hears "over over" in "flowering over" such that neither seen colors nor imagined colors has dominance one over the other. The citrons are the familiar fruit of the "Land of the Lemon Trees" that grow out of the reading process.

Shifting from color to synaesthesia, I want to explore further how vision is subordinated into a generic sense in Stevens' work. For although visual perception assumes a central place in the poetry, this is precisely because the eye's realism is an object of critique. Stevens' poetry negates the capacity of the eye to reference the world accurately, and meta-corporealizes the visual into a synaesthetic harmony in which all sensory effects—sight, hearing, touch, taste, smell—are equally virtual, and received into the body as such. Cook insightfully observes that Stevens' "relentless synaesthesia does not heighten the sense effects but dissipates them" (Cook, 275). Indeed, part of the appeal of synaesthesia for Stevens is its underlying negation of the senses through the fragmentation and isolation of each sense.

Synaesthesia, defined as the "phenomenon wherein one sense modality is felt, perceived, or described in terms of another,"[42] is predicated upon the discrete differences between the five senses. The crossovers between the categories of sight, hearing, touch, taste and smell, foreground the separate qualities of each sense. Yet scholarship on Keats, Baudelaire, and Dickinson (the acknowledged masters of synaesthesia in the century when it notably emerges in poetic practice) as well as I.A. Richards' analysis in *Principles of Literary Criticism*,[43] tends to cast synaesthesia as a way of harmonizing the five senses. To my reading, synaesthesia loses its edges when cast in terms of sensory unity, for wholeness is only one part of the effect.

Stevens echoes Baudelaire's "Au Lecteur" and "L'Invitation au Voyage" in "Sea Surface Full of Clouds," by his use of French refrains, "*C'était mon enfant . . .*" and "*C'était mon frère. . . .*" The sensuousness of the poem renders the comparison inevitable, even without Stevens' deliberate invocation, but the juxtaposition also highlights how the modern American poet begins to swerve away from the nineteenth-century French poet's mystical metamorphosis "De tous mes sens fondus en un" ("Toute Entière").[44] For as with his poetics of color, Stevens fosters a primitive lexicon of the senses such that what is communicated is not a rich texture of sensuous language, but the bare presence of words. There are 143 instances of "eye" in Stevens' work, and 43 instances each of "ear" and "touch." Other frequently appearing words include "sight," "see," "seen," "sees," "sound," "hear," "heard," "taste," "sense," and "senses."[45] The function of such words is distinctly not, as it is in Richards' account, to evoke palpable sensations recollected from past somatic experience. The broad naming of the categories of sense, rather, strips down Baudelairean sensuousness, and calls attention to remoteness, and the hollowness of the gap between past sensation and the present experience of sensory lack.

The severance of the senses, from language, from the human subject, and one from another, most explicitly appears in the poem, "Arcades of Philadelphia the Past" (*CP*, 225). A narrator condemns the nostalgic recollection of past sensations—as of "the strawberries once in the Apennines"—as a form of sensory poverty: "Only the rich remember the past / . . . There they sit holding their eyes in their hands." Stevens puns on "eyes," poking at how the rich derive their identity (their "I's") from an impoverished relation to original sensations: actual travel lacking in the imagination component the poet so values. Stevens would convert sense into a present-tense experience that does not rely upon the crutch of memory and the mimetic access to previous, actual sensations.

The senses are contrasted against each other in a process of negative synaesthesia: one sense modality (sight) is perceived in terms of another (touch), such that the image of "eyes" in "hands" accentuates sensory division and impasse. The monotonous listing of each of the five senses, as of the European cities of Stevens' imaginative itinerary, evacuates their particular content, and no image can be conjured in the "eye" of the reader: "To see / To hear, to touch, to taste, to smell, that's now / That's this." The doubled deictic "That's this" points language back upon itself, converting two indexical adjectives into nouns, and thus creating a noun-sensical now. And the serial listing of the senses orders them into an un-conditioned conditionality, a verbal tense that indicates the indicative.

Stevens generates a primitive anti-synaesthesia by listing the names for each sense: "To see, to hear, to touch, to taste, to smell." The numbing immediacy of these words does produce a unity, but it is a unity based on paradox—one experiences sense as the absence of any particular sense. "Arcades" develops an embittered critique of optical hegemony and the poverty of having a single, privileged sense. When the senses are recirculated for a third time in the poem, it is with an edge of irony that the eye is revealed as divisively trashing the other senses: "The tongue, the fingers, and the nose / Are comic trash, the ears are dirt, / But the eyes are men in the palm of the hand." The poem's last stanza begins with the bitter interrogative, "This?" in an expression of disbelief that the rich are satisfied with the eye alone, that merely indexical and egotistical "single sense." This is the poet lashing out against a postcard relation to the past, and the impoverished notion that sight-seeing offers an integrated version of sensation and imagination—the only meaningful experience of place Stevens' poetry claims.

The poem generates its interpretive difficulty from the overlap of a critique of the "eye" with a critique of all modern sensory experience. The subject's detachment from the sensory "now" is tied to an internal division, in which it is possible to see without seeing, or to speak without hearing. Such lines as "they never hear the past" or "Do they touch the thing they see . . . ?" point to the lack within a particular way of hearing or touching, not merely to an idea that seeing drowns out the other senses. The overlapping of Stevens' actual Pennsylvania past with the assumed, fictional recollections of Italian strawberries points to a more personal impetus for this critique. For Stevens' generic sense poses a challenge to the particular, actual sensations of the non-vicarious tourist.

Stevens uses metaphor to critique metaphor, as Altieri has argued,[46] the eye to critique the eye, and color to critique color. The paradox of sense is conveyed through the very language of sense: the oxymoron of "he smells clouds," since cloud vapor lacks a distinguishable scent; the visual contrast and similitude in "to see the sea"; and the Keatsian opposition of sounds, one heard and one not-spoken, within one: "To hear himself and not to speak." In the final line of "Arcades," the narrator converts the objectionable sensory nostalgia of "The strawberries once in the Apennines" into see-through, non-imagery ("clear") and negative tactility ("scratched"). The photograph is exposed, the rich tourist's nostalgic sensations are revealed as false: "The mountains are scratched and used, clear fakes."

Stevens experiments with synaesthesia more indulgently, and with a less explicit effort at sensory negation, in "Poem Written at Morning." This poem also appears in *Parts of a World*, composed 1937–42, the book most often critically assessed for its lack of internal cohesiveness. Part of Stevens' restraint is bound up in a resistance to synthesize parts: when the world appears as already integrated, the poet's effort becomes one of reasserting parts. The frequency with which Stevens uses "it" generates confusion as to what "it" is, thus splitting the possibilities for reference, and returning pronouns back into nouns: "A sunny day's complete Poussiniana / Divide it from itself. It is this or that / And it is not" (*CP*, 219). Division is at once asserted and negated; "not" itself becomes the principal negative zone in which metaphor is exposed as construct, and sensory perception as poetic artifice. The demonstrative claim, "By metaphor you paint / A thing," is followed in the same stanza by a resistance to generate transparent, vivid imagery. Stevens opts for bad "painting" such that the adjectives "thorned and palmed and blue" are divided as much as connected by "and"; the words alienate as much as vivify the reader's relation to the thing. "Leather" and "Pewter" underscore how unnatural the fruit is: barely still-life.

Not surprisingly, critics of Stevens tend to neglect the poem, although the poem pivots on the rewriting of a significant question of representation. Note the shift between the phrase "By metaphor you paint / A thing" and "The senses paint / By metaphor"; in the latter, "you" the reader are replaced by "the senses," and the "thing" drops out. There is no longer a named pineapple, but a synaesthetic consumption of a fruit-interior through the three most corporeal of the senses: taste, touch, and smell. "The juice was fragranter / Than wettest cinnamon. It was cribled pears / Dripping a morning sap" (*CP*, 219). In these echoes of a classically Keatsian sensuousness, the juice is being described, and the pears are merely "cribled" metaphor. At the associative intersection of "cobbled," (clumsily put together), "cribbed" (stolen, plagiarized, in an infant's bed), and "crippled," this Stevensian non-sense word exposes the artificiality of the American poet's attempt to paint "pairs" through a metaphorics of sense. In a comic encounter of old world sensibility and new world verbal artifice, here Poussin meets Louisiana ("Poussiniana"); the suffix "iana" connotes the parts of a collection, not a Poussin, but the odds and ends related to and by Poussin. The shifts between juice, fragrance, fluidity, taste, texture, sweetness are punningly revealed as "morning sap": the poet's drippingly overwrought desire to conjure sensation itself in some organic presence of form.

Stevens' gesture is self-conscious and it is not; "morning" here is not to be mistaken as a nostalgic "mourning" for lost sense. This is a generic "poem" written by a generic "writer" at a generic "morning." The poem even lacks a particular subject—is it the pineapple? the juice? Stevens wants a general arrival at "the truth," but the abstract truth can only be known through the sense of it: "The truth must be / That you do not see, you experience, you feel" (*CP*, 219). The feeling of "Poem Written at Morning," is not a negative indulgence of mourning, but a positive excess of sensory effects. Like many of the poems of *Parts of World*, it oscillates between the organic and the artificial, as yet unresolved as to how to grow from/build on its Keatsian roots. The clumsy pairing of the two produces the poem's final absurdity: "Green were the curls upon that head." The upward growth of the eye, like grass, produces the green curls of the sensate mind.

AIX-EN-PROVENCE

Eleanor Cook characterizes "skreak" and "skritter," as they appear in the sonnet-length "Autumn Refrain" (1931), as making up one of the noisiest lines in Stevens' poetry. It is worth noting that such "noise" in Stevens coincides with an intent focus on the absence of sound. To maximize the sound effect of silence in this poem, Stevens turns the ear towards one of the most basic elements of poetry: repetition. Given what has thus far been observed about Stevens' use of solid, primary colors to subvert the power of the eye, and the numbing immediacy of negative synaesthesia ("to see, to hear, to touch . . ."), this turn toward sound repeats the paradox of presence and absence at the structural center of Stevens' art of sensory foreclosure.

"Autumn Refrain" can be read, as John Hollander artfully does, as a foreclosure not from sound, but from Keatsian sound. Hollander observes wryly that "There are in America neither larks nor nightingales of the kind that have astonished English poets for their invisible voices; there are only copies of the poems about them."[47] The notion of the American poem as the copy of the English poem explains some of Stevens' desire to convert the discourse of "meta" into a virtue. Indeed, the poem's significant repetition of "I have never—shall never hear" that bird, might as well serve as the refrain haunting this chapter, the prescience of what was to become fact. At the age of 53, when he wrote "Autumn Refrain," Stevens was still holding out for the possibility of European travel, still far from writing, as he did in 1950 to his Parisian correspondent, "But, alas, I have no expectation of ever visiting Europe" (L, 698).

Stevens' rewriting of Keats is significantly evident in a passage from a letter to Barbara Church in the summer of 1948, in which he relays a vicarious experience of the South of France. His sudden transition between Aix-en-Provence and New Haven reveals a crucial alteration of British Romantic sensuousness.

> Some books came recently wrapped in a Paris newspaper which contained photos of some fountains at Aix, not great things, but enough to make a little sound as one walked by. This makes me think of a wild dove that was sitting up on a wire near home a few mornings ago cooing about nothing much. I stopped to look at her. She turned around so she could see me better but went right on with her talk (L, 610).[48]

From the imagination of the actual sound of the fountain in Aix—with its implied severance from any original fountain—Stevens pivots to the actual sound of a visible bird in New Haven. This strange turn is comprehensible only when read against the lines of Keats' "Ode to a Nightingale," from which Stevens draws his associations: "O, for a draught of vintage! that hath been / Cooled a long age in the deep-delved earth, / Tasting of Flora and the country green, / Dance, and Provençal song, and sunburnt mirth! / O for a beaker full of the warm South . . . ."[49] Keats provides the Provençal song and the cool, poetically intoxicating liquid that Stevens associates with photographs of the fountains at Aix-en-Provence. But Keats' foreclosure from seeing the nightingale in "Ode to a Nightingale" is met by Stevens' American foreclosure from ever seeing a nightingale. Keats has memories and originary sensations of nightingales, whereas Stevens has only second-order sensations produced by language and photographs. This absence of original sensations is doubled back upon itself to produce its own positive sensation. Here poetry and photography, rather than contradictory, are structurally conflated; both are sites for feeling the presence of absence. Stevens finds a means to enact the foreclosure which technology, and his adherence to his native soil, accentuate, and to adapt this lack into a linguistic resource.

Stevens converts his foreclosure from actually hearing or seeing, in the face of the Aix photo, into the one positive experience available: the imagination of real sound. The vicarious presence of the fountains is "enough to make a little sound as one walked by." What follows is an associative leap, at once toward and away from Keats, to the real presence of a visible, singing, American wild dove. This is not a non sequitur, but a logical equation, in which imagined sound = visible bird. From the doubled negation of photograph and fountain at Aix comes the positive experience of the actual bird. This dove, cooing about nothing, looks back at him, not unlike the way that silent, seemingly senseless language can look back at its readers, and produce sounds. The wild dove and "Autumn Refrain" are two opposite—not opposed, but doublesided—products of the American poet.

Since Stevens cannot add to Keats' poem, what he can do is generate the doubled sense of lack. Sounds, syllables, words, and phrases, when repeated, introduce a degree of self-reference that Stevens would maximize in order to expose the lack (the felt silence) within sound. Rosu observes how the opposition of silence and sound in "Autumn Refrain" is inscribed only to be dissolved. The "real" sounds of the poem appear in the first line— "The skreak and skritter of evening gone"—as already gone. And the lost sound of the nightingale emerges through the layers of negation as what is not being heard. "Reduced to a residuum, surviving only as a memory of their immediacy," Rosu writes, "the real sounds become virtual fictions themselves, even as the song of the nightingale begins almost to take on reality in the silence that the speaker so intently listens to."(Rosu, 72) The virtual-actual crossroads in "Autumn Refrain" are difficult to locate only because they are everywhere, dispersed in the overlapping patterns of repetition. In the first seven lines of the poem, there is a triple repetition of "gone," of "moon," and of "name."

> The skreak and skritter of evening gone
> And grackles gone and sorrows of the sun,
> The sorrows of sun, too, gone . . . the moon and moon,
> The yellow moon of words about the nightingale
> In measureless measures, not a bird for me
> But the name of a bird and the name of a nameless air
> I have never—shall never hear. (*CP*, 160)

Sound is gone ("skreak and skritter"), birds are gone ("grackles"), and sorrows are gone ("sorrows of the sun"). Yet not only are "skreak and skritter" present to the *reading* ear, but "grackles" also generate a sharp sound effect, communicating the presence of language over and against the absence of the signified birds. The "nightingale" is too mellifluous both as a name and as a bird. The poem needs a name for an American counterpart to Milton or Keats' nightingale, more a word than a bird, that is beaked, black, and crackles in the ear. The challenge seems to be one of finding words with rough edges that can grate against the evasiveness of loss.

Lacking that harsh sensory effect, "sorrows of the sun" and "moon" are difficult to articulate except in a kind of stutter. For as with the "nightingale," language here borders on a romantic lexicon that is more absorptively engaged in longing and mourning over impasse. Unlike Keats, Stevens must abstract the emotion, and name sorrow rather than feel it. Foreclosed from the directionality of address that is possible in "Ode to a Nightingale," or "Ode on a Grecian Urn," this speaker eliminates a "thou." Stevens' poem reworks the oft-heard lines of Keats: "what thou among the leaves hast never known, / . . . Here, where men sit and hear each other groan / . . .Where but to think is to be full of sorrow." The speaker of "Autumn Refrain" is denied the "here" of Keats' poem, unable from his position as an American poet to hear the bird. The address to the "nightingale" confirms the speaker's foreclosure, proving an exercise in linguistic frustration: ". . . not a bird for me / But the name of a bird and the name of a nameless air / I have never—shall never hear." Names and their negation take the place of heard sound, substituting the word-as-presence for the poetic expression of absence or longing. Even the pathos of a construction such as "have never—shall never" is drowned out by the lexical confusion as to what is not being heard. "Air" is a paradox of the silent and the sung: the gaseous nothingness all around us (colorless, odorless, soundless), what a soloist sings without accompaniment, and what Stevens writes as "heir" to Keats. Likewise, the word "bird," without the accompanying illusion of heard melodies, sounds out the paradox.

What drives the poem's refrain of words, phrases, lines, at intervals (the primary inflection of "refrain") is evident if one re-inflects the title to hear "Autumn Refrain" as a seasonal refraining from summer's absorption in the senses, and further, the poet's refrain from a certain kind of speech—from words that lack the tenuousness, the virtuality, and the silence within heard sound. Cook hears a fear of false voice, as well as the fear of silence which current readings (getting it backwards, for the poem manifests a desire to hear silence) hear in the poem. Evident in the trademark refrain of autumn and winter in Stevens' poetry is the seasonal negation of the senses, and this is here tied to a desire to negate false voice, and to experience the resurgence of pure voice through the articulations of silence. For even writing about not hearing the nightingale still generates some kind of sound. The speaker who has never, and shall never, hear the song of the nightingale, still repeats the word "nightingale" (twice) and "bird" (three times). In the dash between "I have never—shall never hear," an unwritten, elided "here" asserts itself against the temporal foreclosures.

Through the negation of everything else, of everything gone, is the non-figurative "something" that resides. Although the sonnet's second "measure" cannot be named or measured as a Pertrarchan sestet because it spans more than six lines, it does register a modulation into another key, in which words achieve something through their repetition.

> And yet beneath
> The stillness of everything gone, and being still,
> Being and sitting still, something resides,
> Some skreaking and skrittering residuum,
> And grates these evasions of the nightingale
> Though I have never—shall never hear that bird.
> And the stillness is in the key, all of it is,
> The stillness is all in the key of that desolate sound. (*CP*, 160)

"Skreaking" and "skrittering" are re-sounded from the first line as continuous modifications of what resides, rather than what is gone. Drawing upon the etymology of "reside" (from the Latin *re*, again or back + *sedere*, to sit), Stevens generates a backward and residual motion to "Being and sitting still." If repetition disrupts the progression of signification, it asserts the presence of the word or the name in its own right. By a backwards conversion, repetition distills the nameless and measureless. It converts the hollowness that cannot be found in technological sensory presence, but is there nonetheless. The reliance upon absence that is at the structural mechanical core of modern experience—belonging also to the photo-side of the postcard even as the actual visual content disguises this absence—is what Stevens would have his readers understand as the structural center of poetry. Further, he means to show over and over that what is not embraced in technology *is* embraced in poetry, and as such, is a positive experience of the absence within words.

His sonnet thus strives to utter its own self-reflexivity, such that "these evasions" refers back to itself, and "the key" is all in the isolated linguistic experience. Evading the object, in this case the "nightingale," by asserting that it cannot be heard, is also critically to evade the absorptive illusion that sounds, other than the words of the poem, can be heard through the medium of the poem. Stevens wants the words to sit forever still (repeating "still" or "stillness" five times) such that the readers can hear them grate and groan against each other, beneath their silent context. Only through the repetitions of what is not, of everything gone, including loss itself, can the newly spawned last two words emerge against the absence of "that bird," asserting their negative presence as "desolate sound."

CHAPTER II

Binocular Optics: Elizabeth Bishop

POSTCARDS

In the vivid account of postcards in Bishop's haunting autobiographical story of 1953, "In the Village," the adult narrator recalls from her early childhood in Nova Scotia holding in her hands "a big bundle of postcards" before she knows how to read. These are not ordinary postcards, but have little crystal flecks outlining the pictured buildings that flake off and glitter in her hands: "some have lines of metallic crystals on them—how beautiful!—silver, gold, red, and green, or all four mixed together, crumbling off, sticking in the lines on my palms. . . ."[1] Iridescence signals a sublime state of sensory absorption in Bishop's work, a translation of early Biblical influences into a self-generated spiritual state of visible materiality, higher than reading, but inextricably connected to the failures and sensory impasse staged by language. Her childhood encounter with postcards reenacts an experience of *not* being able to read—the written word as a block to understanding—but this is not traumatic, far from it. Dazzling crystal words are written in above the pictured buildings: "Some cards, instead of lines around the buildings, have words written in their skies with the same stuff, crumbling, dazzling and crumbling." And these words written onto the picture side visibly fall onto "specks of hands" in the image, and tangibly *as* specks onto her own hands. The words adhere to the child, literally, giving off a sticky meaning felt to be more profound than the linguistic message from which the child is foreclosed. The little girl interprets the written word in the only terms she knows, a self-fashioned method akin to palm reading, in which visual and tactile cues are invested with immense personal meaning. Words circulate for the child, like "stove" and "tears" in "Sestina," as object-like entities that are perceptually, rather than semantically, decipherable. "Speck," and its variant, "fleck," are crucial to Bishop's lexicon despite their seeming negligibility, as black bits that mark the indistinguishable convergence of the visual and verbal signs. Bishop, in the postcard "speck," attempts to squeeze the written message into a visible, tangible, point.

The foreclosure from semantic meaning at the core of the modern American poet's project takes a different spin in Bishop, as it does in the work of her postwar contemporaries such as Lowell, Swenson, and Plath. Each locates in childhood semiotics the access to a sense realm that is idealized, and that, I contend, draws from the technological models of the day to accentuate features of absorption and intense multi-sensory, especially visual, experience. Bishop articulates a wish, like her idealized and occasionally actualized wish to draw, for an enhanced way of seeing; she would have the lines of writing, not on the reverse side of the postcard, but as superimposed exclusively on the image side of the postcard. The adult narrator of "In the Village" comments longingly: "The crystals outline the buildings on the cards in a way buildings never are outlined but should be—if there were a way of making the crystals stick. . . . ." Poetry is an ad hoc method for making the crystals stick, for making the imposing visible reality of modern buildings into an iridescent, desirable, graspable outline. Poetry is the most unlikely "line," which is to say it works against the most impediments. As Lowell writes in "Myopia," "my five senses clenched / their teeth," and how could they not in so blank a medium? [2] Bishop pushes the anguish to the edges in her poetic writing, coasting on the wish that lines—lines on buildings, lines on her palms, and what is not said, lines of poetry—take on a sparkling tactile visibility.

Bishop's efforts to render visible the particular phenomena of a sensuous and everyday world contrast sharply with Stevens' structural effacement of such details, as is evident in their different usage of the place name. Key West, Florida, the island of Stevens' actual travels, and Elizabeth Bishop's off-and-on home from the late 1930s through the 1940s, figures in her work as a prominent source for quasi-visual description. According to Bishop's notes for a poetry reading, her poem "Seascape" (1941) derives from a time when she was "out in a small inboard motorboat, fishing in the evening, in that harbor where Stevens dreamed of living on a houseboat." [3] Evident in this brief account is Bishop's fondness for locating herself, at once literally and figuratively, in liminal places akin to those of the childhood imagination. The overlapping edges of land and water, familiar from "The Map," and the suspension of a little fishing boat in water, as I explore in "The Fish," are characteristic of the half-dry, half-wet settings common to her poetry. By locating Stevens at "evening," marginally between dream and reality, inside and out, small and vast, Bishop foregrounds the structural doubling, and the *sense* of between, that links their two aesthetics. By locating Stevens literally in the same spot, however, amid the sensuous material, flora and fauna, climate and geography of a particular harbor of Key West, Bishop situates the elder poet in a more abundantly referential Key West than his poetry allows. Her statement confirms the strength of her affinity with Stevens, but also exposes her impulse to rewrite his point of view.[4]

Stevens' celebrated poem, "The Idea of Order at Key West," makes a tenuous gesture toward the town ("the lights in the fishing boats at anchor there"), but does not depend upon a readerly sensation of the visible place in the way Bishop's poems seem to. This divide between Stevens and Bishop shows itself in their use of the sublime trope of sunlight and darkness. The two-sidedness of light and dark in Stevens' Rome postcard is precisely the dualism upon which "Seascape" hinges, but whereas for Stevens "words, lines" are aligned with "dark things" (*CP*, 465), words for Bishop operate as lighthouses that illuminate against a fearful darkness.

Bishop conflates a strong glare with strong words in the personified lighthouse of "Seascape." The neurotic lighthouse, in "black and white clerical dress," is Bishop's unlikely spokesperson for a part-celestial, part-earthly sublime light projected in darkness.

> Heaven is not like flying or swimming,
> but has something to do with blackness and a strong glare
> and when it gets dark he will remember something
> strongly worded to say on the subject.[5]

This apparent black and white clarity follows the vacillation of the poem's referent in the first half of "Seascape" between an actual Florida seascape (occupied by Bishop or Stevens, or both-in-one), and a "cartoon by Raphael for a tapestry for a pope," which Bishop had admired at the Vatican Museum in 1937, and remarked to be "very Florida-like."[6] During the same trip to the Raphael Room, Bishop had noted a "miraculous draught of fishes," which, along with the tapestry flora, contributes to the lines, "a fish jumps, like a wild-flower / in an ornamental spray of spray." Whether the spray refers to ocean spray or to a spray of flowers, to Raphael's tapestries or to Key West itself, is answered by the fact that this is a "spray of spray." The word "spray," repeated, enforces a visual order—a simultaneity of surfaces, painted and/or seen—that resists a determinate verbal relation.

Bishop's unblinking attention to visual details, as her poems, "Poem" and "The Fish," attest to in this chapter, draws from the logic of the optic technology that fascinated her. She works to reproduce and outshine the desirable still visual scenes produced by the visual media to which she gravitated: camera obscura, stereoscopes, binoculars, magnifying lenses. Her verbal recreations at moments dazzle with presumed success, at others, are infused with impossibility. The poetic current running throughout is Bishop's attempt to generate an instant of forgetting that distracts from the unreachable, verbally derived, visual referent. She joins a crew of American poets in turning the unattainable and frustrated gestures toward actual sensation in poetry to her advantage.

Foreclosure is Bishop's poignant theme, as she rotates around the goal of an image so technically perfect (and made so by language) that it seems tangible. She recounts through her exposure to optics, especially when linked to childhood experiences, a desire to reach through the apparatus and enter the reality that she sees there. She supplants a version of a modern technological sublime with a verbally-achieved one, but she does so unexpectedly by seeming to efface literary communication and to employ in its stead, technological, optical methods. Two-dimensional visual reality is granted so much central focus that at times Bishop's works seem to spring free from the intense verbal consciousness in which she suffers and excels. Of course her efforts to create a feeling of heightened optic precision are impeded by the uniquely verbal basis of the poetic medium: seemingly extra-sharp imagery cannot be maintained, and at the moment when words cease to act as viewing optics, the readerly sensation is one of an awareness of words. The project resembles Stevens' own, but Bishop's tactic for achieving the sensation of words is quite opposite. The reflexivity works not to blind the medium, as in Stevens, but to shed an awareness of the failings of poetic sight. To see a "spray of spray," is to see two-in-one, a simultaneity of flower and fish, that forces the paradox of sight in poetry, and the accompanying recognition of the failure of sight, as in Stevens' work, as a positive experience.

The contemporary reader is ideally situated for the kinds of tricks, cues, and manipulative mimesis Bishop has in store, trained by mechanical optics to moments of intense perceptual absorption and attention. Bishop profits from the situation of the twentieth century subject by preoccupying the attention such that uncertainty as to what we are seeing, and the disjunctions within the visible scene, do not prompt the question: how are we seeing through an opaque medium at all? Non-visible content is forced to the periphery. Even as interrogatives are important components of Bishop's poetry,[7] answers are relegated to language's blind spot: "There is no way of telling," she writes, "The Eyes say only either" (*CP*, 74). In a dazzling superimposed image of "Seascape," Bishop brilliantly edges the leaves of ordinary sight with still more empirical detail: "bright green leaves edged neatly with bird-droppings / like illumination in silver" (*CP*, 40). The black and white bird guano, as much word- as bird-droppings, neatly edged (etched?) on two-dimensional leaves, forms a third, celestial dimension of silver. By manipulating and overlapping two-dimensional surfaces into an illusion of depth and visibility, Bishop creates the impression of a veritable and material "See-scape." Her verbal effects are at once extra-visual and unretreatingly optical; a sublime of ordinary seeing in a medium that always, structurally, is also radically foreclosing sight.

In an August 1946 review of Bishop's first book, *North & South*, Edward Weeks writes that roughly half the poems can be categorized as "straight descriptive verse, much of it growing out of the author's experience in Florida. . . ."[8] The high proportion of directives to *see* in Bishop's verse prompts this common early response to her work. "Florida," in her poem of that title, more than a name (even as it is introduced as "The state with the prettiest name"), is a real place of mangrove roots, palm trees, tanagers, pelicans, and shell varieties. But as recent Bishop criticism amply observes, her visual scenes are far from "straight,"[9] as the most apparently descriptive poems are always displaced from an actual scene in some way, whether by particular angles or shifting perspectives, close-up or miniature views, the peculiarity of chosen details, or by their status as secondary representations of paintings or minor art works. "Florida" is no exception, for Bishop presents not a picture-perfect view, but as in "The Bight," a skeletal, exposed, decaying scene featuring large eye-sockets of turtle skulls, circling buzzards, and a rotted, sagging coast-line.

This dark underside of Florida turns literally dark as Bishop shifts the description to Florida "after dark." Precisely where Stevens denies the image-face of the postcard, substituting it with the verbal reality of "Rome after dark" (confirming his disposition for imaginary travel), Bishop abundantly and almost exclusively satisfies the postcard's picture side (confirming her life-long passion for actually living in exotic places). Bishop describes in detail what the eyes literally see of Florida after dark:

> After dark, the fireflies map the heavens in the marsh
> until the moon rises.
> Cold white, not bright, the moonlight is coarse-meshed,
> and the careless, corrupt state is all black specks
> too far apart, and ugly whites; the poorest
> post-card of itself. (*CP*, 33)

In the classical tradition of *enargeia*, Bishop creates vivid effects of fireflies, moonlight, whites and blacks—Florida illuminated—and in so doing reaches past the constraints of language to produce a visible scene. But the result is a flawed postcard reproduction: Florida as "the poorest postcard of itself." Bishop's postcard is at odds with Stevens', for where Stevens would prove himself a mimesis-resistant poet, Bishop strives for a kind of supermimesis, in which the sensation of imitation slipping away produces its own reality effect. She often facilitates this process, again paradoxically, by tipping the sensation of real images toward imitation; the copy is given an enhanced reality effect, while the reality of the Florida referent diminishes. Florida becomes more itself as its own bad copy, visible through gradations of partial light, loss of color, and obscure details of texture and proportion. The state is flattened into a coarse, black-and-white image while the postcard is vivified into a seemingly sensory state.

In this doubled view of Florida after dark, in which state and postcard overlap in a faulty superimposition, an additional view appears, that of writing itself: "all black specks / too far apart, and ugly whites." At the same time that we are seeing Florida at night by its natural illuminants, we are literally *seeing* printed letters as they fail to produce a coherent, seamless, actual picture. Dovetailed with the natural factors that make Florida difficult to see (i.e., nighttime) is the unnatural strength of linguistic artifice that renders Florida visible through the poem. At this juncture, Bishop gives us not a black-out, after Stevens' example, but a visible materialization of *writing* Florida as a bad postcard. As in "Seascape," the effort to see particulars in the face of ambiguity reaches a certain breaking point at which a particulate, colorful scene reverts to a coarse black and white. The visual thematics of decay in "Florida" prefigure this turn toward Bishop's counterintuitive casting of her blind spot as visibility; the failures, obscurities, and slippages of superimposition act as the visible registers of language's poverty to produce real images.

Bishop's binocularity does not admit a division of image-face and writing-face; the two faces are not back-to-back, as we saw in Stevens' Rome postcard, but superimposed. They can flip back to being separate extremes, but the postcard analogy is apt only insofar as it is revised as the superimposition of reading and seeing. The driving impulse of the verbal-visual relation is toward an impossibly seamless fusion. Bishop's own analogue is the optic apparatus. Accounts of binoculars, microscopes, stereoscopes and other material, optical instruments are scattered throughout her letters, poems, and prose writings. The water droplets, prisms, mirrors, glass, and tears that are familiar motifs, particularly in *North & South,* function as incomplete optics, but are also significant insofar as they provide a stage for both impeded and heightened seeing. Bishop's binocularity (binocular from *bini* "two together" and *oculus* "eye") derives from the effort to have poetry do two things at once, to see with a reading eye, and to read with a seeing eye, the kind of paradox that can promote "fleck" or "speck" to exalted moments in the verse. Properties of magnification, hypervisuality, distortion and inversion, perspectival constraints, and enhanced depth perception, act as the visible registers for the imperfect superimposition of a binocular reading eye and seeing eye.

In an early Florida notebook, Bishop entitles a projected essay, "Grandmother's Glass EYE—an Essay on Style." The idea was important enough for Bishop to recover it some forty years later, in a Guggenheim application:

> Quite often the glass eye looked heavenward, or off at an angle, while the real eye looked at you . . . The situation of my grandmother strikes me as rather like the situation of the poet: the difficulty of combining the real with the decidedly un-real; the natural with the unnatural; the curious effect a poem produces of being as normal as sight and yet as synthetic, as artificial, as a *glass eye*.[10]

The two eyeballs are striking as a bizarre image of an art-life hybrid. Their seemingly material curiosity covers over a deeper, structural curiosity: that Bishop, a writer, thinks about poetic style in visual terms. Even in the most recent critical reception of her work, this proves a sticking point to reading her work. For her elusive brilliance, while pretending to a modest, descriptive project, lies in her attempts to stretch poetry beyond its verbal limits. In the above passage, Bishop manages to slip in the strange, Emersonian gesture of turning the "I," and the poem along with it, into the image of a detached eyeball (or, two eyeballs detached from each other). Bishop's "curious effect," other than the named one, is that she asks us to contemplate *what* we are seeing to the exclusion of the fact *that* we are seeing.

Her subtle trap is to do this by conflating metaphors for seeing with actual seeing. To avoid this trap, it is important not to swallow completely Bishop's analogy with optics, not to imagine as she would have us do, that her poems *are* optics and correspond physiologically to the eye. Rather, I contend in this chapter that Bishop maintains a position of analytic and critical concentration within the empirical, visual effects of a sensuous, everyday, as well as historically, technologically situated world. The following sections are organized around optical instruments that stage a particular problem in dual seeing: the necessity of a seemingly monocular, fixed view in the camera obscura; uncertainty of depth perception and hyperreality effects in the stereoscope; seeing through magnification what cannot be seen at all with the eye alone. The overarching theory of binocularity, explored in the final section in tandem with Barthes' theory of the reality effect, relies upon the notion that the prismatic visual effects of Bishop's poems are produced by the simultaneous inflation and diminishment of the eye, where the enhanced eye must see through the diminished eye (the real eye through the glass eye). In this model, the reader's awareness of making language "see," against its own logic, is elided, only to return as language's positive sensation of real images.

CAMERA OBSCURA

Bishop read Newton's *Opticks* (1704) several years after graduating from Vassar, during the period in which she composed the short stories, "The Sea & Its Shore" (1937) and "In Prison" (1938). Both stories literalize the fantasy of withdrawing to a space akin to a camera obscura, a shack or a prison cell, that constrains the subject to useless acts of reading and seeing. Newton's "dark Chamber," among other seventeenth- and eighteenth-century philosophical and scientific accounts of the camera obscura, shares several of the features significant to Bishop's formula. An enclosed space with a narrow opening to an outside world of real images, light passing through a prism or conduit, the trope of sunlight and darkness, and the necessity of observer passivity, all form part of the same, desirable complex.[11]

In a very dark Chamber, at a round hole, about one third Part of an Inch broad, made in the shut of a window, I placed a glass prism, whereby the Beam of the Sun's Light, which came in at that Hole, might be refracted upwards toward the opposite wall of the chamber, and there form a coloured image of the Sun.[12]

Newton's "I" throughout the *Opticks* is charged with his sense of ingenuity at setting up an experimental apparatus.[13] The contrast between active investment in the details of physically setting up a dark box or chamber, and the passivity, and eventual elision, of human participation that the experiment entails, is recognizably the very contrast struck by Bishop's narrators.

Why is the camera obscura an attractive model for Bishop? An early optic that gained prominence in the late 1500's and a precursor to the modern camera, the camera obscura projects an image of an external, objective scene through a lens or aperture (not prism) onto a screen inside the apparatus. It is the privileged instance of a seventeenth and eighteenth-century geometrical optics in Jonathan Crary's critical history of vision technologies.[14] Even as it prescribes a fixed site for the "viewer" as an abstract position, it does not require the presence of a person in order to operate. The human body can come and go, is effectively disposable, once the apparatus is in place. Bishop is likely drawn to this model, especially early on, because its geometrical status overstates a sense of stability: the promise of a safe, unchanging perspective from which to view the world that does not require an "author." Insofar at it confirms Renaissance perspective and the existence of an objective field of vision, the camera obscura is similar to other instruments of interest to Bishop, such as the telescope, microscope, periscope, and binoculars.

Of course monocularity is an illusion in this most escapist version of Bishop's optics, for the fixed permutation of observer, optic, and field of vision fluctuates between a triangular and dual structure. The body of the observer is a floating term, neither inside the dark chamber, nor wholly outside of it. This is the situation of the narrator of "In Prison," who fantasizes the exact measurements of a prison cell, and the placement of a window view, without ever *realizing* his fantasy within the story. His giddy pleasure at the prospect of slipping, not out of control, but into a precisely controlled space where requirements are made to see one fixed view, derives from a counter-intuitive conception of freedom as the physical containment of sensory impressions. This is a version of the real that begins only when a set of literal constraints are imposed that radically narrow the activities of seeing (and, vicariously, reading).

One critic introduces the term "paradoxical prisons" to point to the underlying contradictions of Bishop's work, citing the would-be prisoner's Kantian motto, "Freedom is the knowledge of necessity."[15] Craving to be freed into mental and imaginative faculties by physical containment—the necessity of a literal space with only the most narrow opening onto the world—Bishop's narrator does not expect fully to realize his faculties until imprisonment begins. Displaced onto the narrator's desires are Bishop's own desires that her poems be required to "see" what it is immediately before the eyes (and concurrently, that mental activities such as remembering, emoting, or thinking be forced to the periphery, or, as in "One Art," to the parenthetical). The camera obscura, at once enhancing the visual capacities of the observer, and threatening to efface the observer altogether, radically narrows the kind of activity the human subject engages in. Bishop, surprisingly, finds reason to exult in this technical necessity:

> I should like a cell about twelve or fifteen feet long by six feet wide. The door would be at one end, the window, placed rather high, at the other, and the iron bed along the side. . . . About the view from the window: I once went to see a room in the Asylum of the Mausoleum where the painter V— had been confined for a year. . . what chiefly impressed me was the view . . . . A row of cypresses stood at the right. It was rapidly growing dark . . . but I can still see as clearly as in a photograph the beautiful completeness of the view from that window: the shaven fields, the black cypress, and the group of swallows posed dipping in the gray sky. . . . (*Prose*, 185–186)

Confinement is given three literal, physical dimensions: the prison cell (its actual measurements), the framed window view, and the painter confined to an asylum, referred to as "V." The missing physical dimension is that of Vincent van Gogh, as Bishop significantly elides the name of the painter in her "literal" portrait (literal here in the sense of *littera*, a letter of the alphabet). Instead, the painter is incorporated into the physical text: the letter "V" and its doubling in "W" are embedded in the phrase, "view from the window," as well as "shaven fields" and "group of swallows." By such techniques of embedding, Bishop reinserts the invisible subject or authorial presence, her "I," as we will see her do in "The Fish."

Iconographically, the letter "V" signals a two-pointed view that narrows to a single point, or inversely opens out. The camera obscura may promise a monocular set-up, but the view it actually stages is doubled and even tripled in this narrative account. The reader projects an uncertain double-view, like in "Seascape": either a real scene, or by ekphrasis, a Van Gogh painting. What we are seeing is made still more ambiguous by the phrase, "clearly as in a photograph," for the view now appears as a black-and-white photograph as well. The fantasy of monocularity—of being "one-eyed"—is undermined by the dividing perspectives of the too literal "V." The swallows as inversions of the v-shaped crows of Van Gogh's *Wheatfield with Crows*, the shaven fields of his Provençal paintings superimposed upon the shaven ear with which he paid for them, and the prison cell like a mausoleum tomb, convey the macabre aspect of the narrator's delight in this gray view. The cherished window view is purchased at the cost of the human body; when a poem acts as a camera obscura, a dark chamber for receiving images, the author elusively slips away.

When the camera obscura is invoked more explicitly, in Bishop's account of Boomer's chamber in "The Sea & Its Shore," it is preceded by an extended comparison between the flight of old newspaper sheets along the beach and the flight of birds. Unlike the birds, the papers have no discernible goal: "If any manner was their favorite, it seemed to be an oblique one, slipping sideways" (*Prose*, 174). The narrator's identification with the sideways flight of newspaper, slipping away from its news content, focuses into a binocular image: "The fold in the middle of the large news sheets acted as a kind of spine, but the wings were not coordinated" (*Prose*, 175). Bishop attempts a visible image of her writing style, through a flattening of the romantic bird image into a sheet of paper with two uncoordinated wings. Unlike Stevens' version of two-sidedness, Bishop's printed words are folded visibly together into a single paper-thin image, and the slippages between word and image are visualized as literal flight problems.

Boomer's liminal positioning between modern material life and a life of the imagination—a garbage collector by trade, a dreamer and proto-postmodern collage artist by inclination—may point to his special status as a modern figure with a retroactive, romantic sensibility. Boomer discovers a newspaper poem, markedly romantic in style, that uncannily doubles as a description of his one-room house and as an account of a camera obscura: "Much as a one-eyed room, hung all with night," it begins in mock-Shakespearean, "*Only that side, which adverse to the eye / Gives but one narrow passage to the light, / Is spread with some white shining tapestry*" (*Prose*, 178). This "one-eyed room" is as close as Bishop comes stylistically to an artificial syle, but she manages at the same time to articulate her ideal of a poem as a white shining tapestry, a visual tactile glimmering thing. Rather than the announced monocularity, this chamber manifests a complex series of slippages between singularity and plurality that seem to produce, despite the narrow passageway, vivid, albeit flickering, images. "*An hundred shapes that through the flit airs stray,/ Rush boldly in, crowding that narrow way,/ And on that bright-faced wall obscurely dancing play*" (*Prose*, 178). Bishop invokes the trope of black and white, sun and dark, favored by all three poets highlighted in this book, because it marks the impossible convergence of seeing and reading, page and image. The camera obscura is a primitive optical analogy for a writing method that would bring alive a blank wall, and, in the process, distract attention from the writer's apparatus.

Bishop's attraction to instruments that literally constrain seeing, evident in her poems and stories, somewhat surprisingly slips over into her actual life, as documented in her letters. In the summer of 1943, Bishop found a job grinding binocular lenses at the Navy's Optical Shop in Key West.[16] She wrote to Marianne Moore, "of course I could spend a lot of time—had to—watching everything through magnificent optical instruments of every kind, including periscopes." Although she liked the affable sailors whom she worked alongside, she berated them for their lack of imagination and investment in optical theory: "not one of them had any idea of the theory of the thing, why the prisms go this way or that way, or what 'collimate' and 'optical center' really mean. . . ."[17] Her comment to Moore that she "had to" look through "magnificent optical instruments" is partially inflected with her pleasure at this necessity.

That Bishop's interests in optical instruments lean toward pre-twentieth-century inventions—the camera obscura, binoculars, periscopes, telescopes, and microscopes, rather than newer technologies—exposes one aspect of her trope of visual literalism. Each of these instruments precisely demarcates a field of vision from which the observer is physically distinct. Each offers the safety and pleasure of viewing the world from a displaced and mediated position that nonetheless confirms through its visual details the stability of the real. The periscope, to cite Bishop's example, allows the viewer to see through a tube-and-mirror apparatus what would otherwise be out of sight. Typically used from a submerged submarine or behind a physical obstacle, the periscope is constructed on the assumption that the human subject is in a displaced position of not otherwise being able to see anything at all. In this model, withdrawal from the world hinges upon seeing its empirical details.

What proved unnerving in the practical, wartime atmosphere of the binocular factory—that one not only could but had to look through the lenses—is precisely what Bishop craves and struggles to actualize in the artistic realm. Her late poem, "The End of March" (1974), culminates the life-long fantasy of a "crypto-dream-house,"[18] where nothing would be required of one, and where looking through binoculars and reading books would be an entirely useless pastime.

> I'd like to retire there and do nothing
> or nothing much, forever, in two bare rooms:
> look through binoculars, read boring books,
> old, long, long books, and write down useless notes,
> talk to myself, and, foggy days,
> watch the droplets slipping, heavy with light. (*CP,* 179–180)

Although Bishop retracts the fantasy ("perfect! But—impossible"), she momentarily thematizes in the poem what she famously claims in her "Darwin" letter to Stevenson is necessary for the creation and reception of art: "a self-forgetful, perfectly useless concentration."[19] Her interest in the seemingly useless details of books and visual phenomena is bound up with the resistance of such details to meaning. "Nothing" serves as a generic category of experience for which different details and activities can be substituted. But the necessity that there are such details remains structurally central to the experience, as does the fact that these details are scientifically verifiable.

Darwin, in Bishop's transparently autobiographical portrait, is described as a "lonely young man, his eyes fixed on facts and minute details, sinking or sliding giddily off into the unknown." The phrase "eyes fixed on facts" introduces a crucial slippage between seeing and reading; while the eyes are fixed on factual details (the scientific definition of facts as "events under description"), something else is slipping away. A giddy pleasure of uncontrol, and of having placed oneself in a position of having to slip away, accompanies for Bishop the attempt to treat reading/writing as a purely optical process. In aligning the figure of the poet with that of the scientist, Darwin or Newton, Bishop literally instrumentalizes poetry with a technical necessity to see. The failure of metaphorical seeing, and the return of language as its own experience, coincides with the pleasurable illusion that we are technically seeing something.

Early criticism of Bishop, as we began to note, tends to praise her remarkable powers of description and the accuracy of her visual details. Hovering between adulation of the poetry and trivialization of it as merely descriptive, such responses are less critical than they are participatory in the trap of the literal.[20] A more recent strand of criticism, led by Lee Edelman, comprehends literalism as itself a trope. Edelman addresses how literality acts as the crucial figure of Bishop's "In the Waiting Room." The fixed emphasis on the exact issue of the National Geographic which "Elizabeth" encounters—February 1918—actually undermines the stability of the literal; the pains to describe only dramatize "the fundamental 'error' of figurative language." [21] David Jarraway spins Edelman's argument toward the visual, locating in the moment of accuracy "a paradoxical crisis of vision." He makes the clarifying observation: "paradoxically, the purest gauge of what ideally cannot be seen (or seen readily) is what 'the real eye,' in fact, does see and perhaps sees only too well."[22] The paradox is that what is concealed is all too visible, and that what appears with the assurance of scientific verifiability is the least certain.

Costello claims of Bishop that she dismantles the notion of the poet as visionary. Her book-length study of Bishop as a "visual poet" opens with Bishop's demotion of vision to looks—a distinction we will see Bishop herself make in "Poem." [23] "Emerging from a tradition of seeing that idealizes it to Vision," Costello writes, "Bishop's is a poetry of looks;" her poetry rejects the notion of a transcendent gaze in favor of a peripheral, transient look or "glimpse." Costello notes that Bishop neither flinches from the observable world, like a modernist such as Stevens, nor assumes the "camera-like mastery" of the objectivists. Underlying the transient, observational style of Costello's book, linked mimetically to Bishop's style, is the significant argument that Bishop's attempts at visual mastery are a highly ambivalent affair, in which each look poses a different challenge to her own mastery.

The nuance I would add to these interpretations is that Bishop places herself, and vicariously her reader, in a trap in which we have to see something. That sense of necessity driving the poetry, focused as in "The End of March" on "the drab, damp, scattered stones" multicolored in their bezels of sand, may make the reader feel variously boxed in or fixed on visible details, but also privy to a special kind of illumination that occurs only through dark-chambered words. The ending to the translation of Octavio Paz's "Objects & Apparitions," a direct address to the artist, Joseph Cornell, reads: "inside your boxes / my words became visible for a moment." Placed as the penultimate poem in *Geography* III, the poem is clearly important to Bishop's aesthetics. The emphasis on making visible the poet's words is not that of a concrete poet, but of a poet who would create the sensation of visibility through words. Bishop's admission that she would "love to be a painter,"[24] and further, her lament that everything might have been different if she were, points to her desires and expectations about visual realism. Her watercolor paintings are distinctly not abstract, though distinctly not realistic either, detailing subjects familiar to her poetry, such as flowers, landscapes, architecture, and interiors, with a careful attention to detail and the odd perspective. The fixation on the detail, something of Bishop's trademark, is turned in *"Objects & Apparitions"* onto items for trading or passing among hands, visible treasures to be picked up out of the poem, as if from one of Cornell's boxes: "Marbles, buttons, thimbles, dice, / pins, stamps, and glass beads." In the translation, Cornell's boxes become primitive optical apparatuses, a box with four corners in which "shadowless" figures play hide and seek (*CP*, 275). The boxed-in view enhances the illumination and value of the details within, generating a necessity that the objects of exchange be seen rather than touched, in a useless but meaningful transaction not between people, but between reader and artwork.

STEREOSCOPIC VIEW

> each riser distinguished from the next
> by an irregular nervous saw-tooth edge,
> alike, but certain as a stereoscopic view.
> —"Cape Breton" (*CP*, 67)

A new currency in images emerges with the commercialization of the still photograph into the postcard and stereoscope. Evident from Stevens' postcard travels is a novel way to travel while remaining in a comfortable domestic setting. The commodity image brings with it a convergence of travel and domesticity—more than coincidentally, two of the privileged themes in Bishop's work. Bishop delights in mixing up currencies, and in generating exchanges between places, persons, images, and objects as if they are all equivalents. Commercial travel, or travel in commercial images, is often matched, as in a poem like "Filling Station," with comically interpersonal and native details. In the observations of Miss Breen in "Arrival at Santos," or old Mrs. Sennet in her prose piece, "The Housekeeper," a peculiar system of exchange arises whereby visible objects, places, and people are each flattened out, almost commodified like paper money or photonegatives. "Ports are necessities, like postage stamps . . . they seldom seem to care what impression they make," Bishop writes in the first poem of *Questions of Travel* (1965). Santos is one of dozens of ports she came to know well over her decades of sea travel, and it is easy to see how the multiplicity of images produced by modern travel, whether natural views or commercial images, would prompt Bishop to make a comic exchange of one place not with another, but with its postcard ("Florida"), stereoscopic image ("Cape Breton"), or the "impression" produced by a postage stamp ("Arrival at Santos").

Bishop's efforts to domesticate her travel are the reverse of Stevens' travels within domesticity.[25] Whereas Stevens would convert the logic of the commodified still image into a new poetic real, Bishop seizes the occasion to rebalance the real with its commodified copy. In her two-dimensional portrait of "Gregorio Valdes," a little Cuban painter whose "copies of local postcards" stood in a Duval Street cigar factory window in Key West, Bishop transforms an impoverished, marginal "Sign Painter" into a heroic artist who lives a life seamlessly of a piece. She hangs the portrait, so to speak, upon a series of attempts at false three-dimensionality in his work, not unlike the 3-D effects I examine in the O'Hara chapter. Among them are a "real View" with a "tiny figure of a man on a donkey" and the "white speck of a thatched Cuban cabin," the trompe l'oeil of a painted towel rack, and the *mise-en-abyme* of a painting of her Key West house leaning against the house itself (*Prose*, 55). Bishop delights in these near-reality slippages, in which the verisimilitude tricks a person in some cases to act upon double-eye logic.

The self-conscious recognition of the proximity of photo-realism to bad art (perhaps Bishop's own fear regarding supermimesis) is frequently made by her with respect to her actual relatives, uncles in particular, as in the two ekphrastic poems, "Large, Bad Painting" and "Poem," and her short prose memoir, "Memories of Uncle Neddy." In the latter, Bishop tries to trick the reader into three-dimensional presence; the piece is set in an apartment in Rio de Janeiro, from which location Bishop announces: "My Uncle Neddy, that is, my Uncle Edward, is *here*"(228). This is followed by the quick qualification that he is leaning against the wall, at cat-eye level, just back from the framer's. Overcompensation for absence, in part autobiographical because of Bishop's essentially orphaned upbringing, here takes the form of an extra-mediated, comically 3-D, version of human presence.

Another portrait, this time not painted but biographical, is "The Housekeeper," a minor write-up of an acquaintance living in a little Cape Cod cottage. The piece is exceptional for borrowing its interpersonal logic from a commercial optical instrument: the stereoscope. It opens with the domestic activity of two shared looks, and the irregularity of their points of convergence. Bishop's particular interest in "the funny cards" derives from their effect of hyperrealism, linked to distortions of depth perception. The piece begins:

> My neighbor, old Mrs. Sennett, adjusted the slide of the stereoscope to her eyes, looked at the card with admiration, and then read out loud to me, slowly, " 'Church in Marselaze. France.'" Then, "Paris." "Paris," I decided, must be an addition of her own. She handed the stereoscope over to me. I moved the card a little farther away and examined the church and the small figures of a man and woman in front of it. The woman was dressed in a long skirt, a tiny white shirtwaist, and a dot-like sailor hat, and though standing at the foot of the church steps, through the stereoscope she and the man appeared to be at least fifty feet from the church. (*Prose*, 205)

The addition of Paris is a significant bit of fabulation, for it adds an extra "dot-like" place-name to what is already there, undermining the already tenuous stereoscopic claim on a distant point of reference. Mrs. Sennet merely expands upon a tendency, structurally present in the medium, toward overdone, far-fetched realism. The slippage between Paris and "Marselaze" (Marseilles) may be the product of Mrs. Sennet's desires and pretensions, but the slippage in the apparent location of the man and the woman, at once next to the church and fifty feet away, derives from the technical make-up of the instrument. These two kinds of slippage—the technical or literal view overlayed with the personal view—prompts Bishop's exploration of a stereoscopic literary style.

Of Bishop's optics, the stereoscope most foregrounds irregularity and the disjunctive perspectives within an image. Rather than tacitly eliding a third term, the stereoscope foregrounds it. The authenticity of the field of vision is not taken for granted; the observer perceives a tenuous, visual reality that exists only as an extension of his or her own sensory and cognitive processes. Kaja Silverman writes that the stereoscope is "a direct extension of the discovery that the human subject has binocular rather than monocular vision."[26] The principles of the stereoscope correspond to the anatomical structure of the optical chiasma, the point where the nerves connecting the brain and the retina cross. Vividness in the stereoscope increases not where the optic axes converge (that is, with the illusion of a unified field of vision) but where the axes diverge. Objects placed in the near or middle ground serve to derange optical unity, thereby enhancing the effect of three-dimensional solidity.

The stereoscope is Crary's metaphor for a physiological optics emerging in the nineteenth century in which uncertainty about what constitutes the field of vision, and about the eye's capacity to see what is there, is relocated in the unstable, sensate realm of the body. The stereoscopic viewer sees neither of the two actual images present in the instrument, but conjures up a composite, fictive picture-plane. As the imperfect product of binocular vision, this planar, heterogeneous, three-dimensional space precipitates a referential crisis over the capacity to see. The inventors of the stereoscope, according to Crary, sought an exact match of stereoscopic image and object: "the desired effect of the stereoscope was not simply likeness, but immediate, apparent tangibility."[27] Stereoscopic realism, as in Barthes' theories on denotation, is an effect of the failure of a direct encounter between object and simulacrum, rather than of its success.

Little wonder that Bishop has to adjust the focus, literally, of her own view within the stereoscope, not only because it is different from Mrs. Sennet's, but because of the discrepancies within the doubled image. The figures of the man and woman, with the details "dot-like" and "tiny white," easily double as figures for writing. Trying to see figures through the poetic medium, like in the stereoscope, is an effect of the failure of direct encounter, rather than of its success. Bishop invokes the stereoscope later on in "The Housekeeper"; having used it as a narrative stage for the conflation of commercial and domestic looks, she employs it as a stylistic analogy for the surface-depth disjunction in a biographical portrait.

> Mrs. Sennett's face was large and seemed, like the stereoscope cards, to be at two distances at the same time, as if fragments of a mask had been laid over a background face. The fragments were white, while the face around them was darker and the wrinkles looser. The rims of her eyes were dark . . ..

This passage follows the observation that Mrs. Sennet, wearing a turban of "black silk with a white design," recalls eighteenth-century literary figures. A form of bad realism, the doubled view of Mrs. Sennet's face is implicitly linked to the difficulty of writing/seeing a person in black and white, and the effects of emergence and recession produced by the word-image connection. This is a significant move for Bishop to make, for when seeking to represent poetic style or structure, she looks toward a commercial optical instrument. This move informs my reading of her poems as distinctly working in a modern currency of images, even where she invokes a more traditional form of visual representation such as painting.

Ekphrasis is the traditional frame for poetic maneuvering between word and image, and we have already cited a couple of instances of it, in "Seascape" and "In Prison," in which Bishop engages in half-ekphrasis by vacillating between real and painted views. It is vital to the historical situation of Bishop's project that her poems are never fully ekphrastic, but rather that they explore an exchange between at least two kinds of visual perspectives, over and above the verbal perspective necessitated by the medium. Bishop's ekphrastic poems thus often offer a meditation on exchange-value, whereby the poet-observer investigates looking through the eyes of others. The vacillation between her perspective and that of her great-uncle in "Large Bad Picture" and "Poem," as between her own eye and that of the Christian discoverers in "Brazil, January 1, 1502," creates the effect of a coincidence of two looks. The goal of such poems is the instance of illuminated, vivid detail, which the narrator both strives toward and backs away from. To arrive at the desired visibility effect, however momentarily, is to pass through a disparity of viewpoints; a singular perspective does not yield the same reality effect as do conflated perspectives.

"Poem"(1972), titled with a seeming foresight that it would become one of the most discussed in her work, begins with an emphasis on the disparities that block the very effort to see as if with one perspective. It is placed in *Geography* III after "12 O'Clock News," the poem in which side-headings are oddly matched with prose accounts of geographical landslides, industrialization and other disaster news: "*gooseneck lamp*" with, among other phrases, "Visibility is poor," "*typewriter*" with "tiny principality," "*ink-bottle*" with "secret weapon," and "*typewriter eraser*" with "deceptive illumination." From these technical writing instruments logically follows *Poem*, displaced like the "*typewriter*" or "*typed sheet*" from its narrative subject matter; Bishop's emphasis on the word "poem" is on its status as a literal medium. By calling it "Poem" and then proceeding to overlook the poem as subject matter in favor of the visual perspectives of a miniature painting, Bishop would seem to give away her secret weapon. I choose to examine "Poem," designated as her ars poetica poem, because of my sense that Bishop's critics have not yet adequately explored the historical situation of her of irreducibly double, poetic vision.

Ekphrastic structure is signaled as generic to any "poem," or at least to any Bishop poem. In Bishop's version of ekphrasis, however, she disposes of the hierarchy of image over word in favor of reciprocal relations. This reciprocity involves a doubling up of forms of representation, in which the poet-observer is not concerned to compare two forms of art, but to experience the effect of the real. And the desire to experience this image version of the real seems to be bound up in the visual values of technical instruments such as the stereoscope. What Bishop gives us is not an exact reciprocity, but an overlapping of disparate lenses—visual and verbal—by which a composite image is seen. By this point in her poetic development, Bishop is able to describe, as well as to enact, her visual logic (in this case stereoscopic), which justifies my approach of having it precede, and thus elucidate, the reading of her early poem, "The Fish."

In a commodity exchange in which two-dimensional paper values blend with the false dimensionality of technological images, the hold-in-the-hand "Poem" significantly converges a dollar bill face and stereoscope-like views into two analogies for the same poem/painting. In "Poem," metaphor is introduced as a form of economy, in which linguistic compression becomes the site of exchange between two ways of seeing. The dollar as money introduces an alternative, arbitrary logic which the poem does not exactly follow, but which influences the daring leaps Bishop makes.

> About the size of an old-style dollar bill,
> American or Canadian,
> mostly the same whites, gray greens, and steel grays
> —this little painting (a sketch for a larger one?)
> has never earned any money in its life.
> Useless and free, it has spent seventy years
> as a minor family relic
> handed along collaterally to owners. (*CP*, 176)

Rather than describing directly the age, colors, size, indeterminate nationality, and minor value of the painting, Bishop ascribes a reality effect to the dollar bill. Metaphor, instead of remaining merely subordinate to the object source, is thus empowered as a collateral object. Through the parallel of the dollar bill and the painting, language appears to trade in real objects rather than mere images. This inverts the logic of a famous essay on the stereoscope, written by Oliver Wendell Holmes, Sr., in 1859: "matter as a visible object is of no great use any longer, except as the mould on which form is shaped. Give us a few negatives of a thing worth seeing, taken from different points of view, and that is all we want of it. . . ."[28] Bishop's inverted logic, as we have seen in contrast with Stevens', is merely a different version of the same structure: a commercial image currency, in which the visible object is substituted by either photo-realism or a paper-thin viewpoint.

In finding an old attic object, Bishop discovers that it resurfaces in a new system of exchange: the old perspective no longer matches up with the new. Two perspectives from angles a little bit apart, one from the past now in paint, and one currently looking through poetic language, produce the poem's principal focus:

> It must be Nova Scotia; only there
> does one see gabled wooden houses
> painted that awful shade of brown.
> The other houses, the bits that show, are white.
> Elm trees, low hills, a thin church steeple
> —that gray-blue wisp—or is it? (*CP*, 176)

At the tip of the V-shaped looks is the apparently certain "It," which is named Nova Scotia. But "it" is a linguistically indeterminate pronoun, neutral beyond the genders of the two observers, and undermining of the confident assurance of literal recognition. Does "It" refer to the painting or an actual place? Does "that awful shade of brown" refer to the paint from the uncle's brush, or to the paint on the wooden houses in Nova Scotia? Two are conjoined in one, creating the illusion that we are really looking at something, when what we are seeing is ambiguity.

Underscoring Costello's comment that "Awareness of schemata does not block illusion"—meant to refute Gombrich's logic of surface and illusion as mutually exclusive[29]—I want to go a step further to say that awareness of schemata is here employed to enhance the effect of referential illusion. Where the eye focuses on the foreground, the divide between surface and illusion becomes more apparent, even as this divide is registered as a positive visual experience.

> In the foreground
> a water meadow with some tiny cows,
> two brushstrokes each, but confidently cows;
> two minuscule white geese in the blue water,
> back-to-back, feeding, and a slanting stick. (*CP*, 176)

Two ways of seeing one thing, "tiny cows" and "two brushstrokes each," reinforce each other through the vacillation between two kinds of concrete details. The brushstrokes, by an unexpected reversal, are converted from mere signifiers into referents of the poem; "two brushstrokes" refer either to the painter's stroking of the brush, or to the paint strokes already visible on the surface. The wording of "two brushstrokes each" underscores the logic: each is two. Bishop substitutes hierarchy with equivalence, such that one term may contain two equal terms (brushstrokes by hand or in paint) or two terms are exchangeable within a single category of value (brushstrokes=cows). This series of equivalents, similar to Floridian and Raphaelite "spray," works against the grain of the reader's expectation to produce an unexpected sensation. In "Poem," the impressionistic reader might call it surprise or joy—"the little we get for free"—but as a sensation of the real, it might as well mark the "coterminus" of Costello's and Gombrich's two points, in which mutual exclusivity and friction between media *is* the effect.

The reality effects of "Poem" increase when two ways of seeing are held in balance nearly simultaneously. The "two minuscule white geese," even smaller proportionately than the "tiny cows," retain their status as two distinct entities. However, their position in water "back-to-back" points to the blind spot in their proximity; back-to-back, the geese cannot see each other, and further, when feeding, they stick their bodies half in, half out of, the water. With the unusual perception of "a slanting stick" added onto the line, the writer's pen and the painter's brush are placed back-to-back, both stuck half-way into representational process; whether by creation, or recognition, both produce looks that see the wood surface (the piece of Bristol board) or the illusionistic stick within the painting.[30] Unlike a postcard logic in which image and word are back-to-back adversaries, this is a stereoscopic logic: as with the "tiny white" in the two figures in Mrs. Sennet's stereoscope, or the "*gooseneck lamp*" of "12 O'Clock News," Bishop compensates for poor visibility in the poetic medium with displaced, double-distanced, or miniature, but nonetheless "visible," effects.

As the perspectives move "up closer," even within the foreground, the angle of the "slanting stick" is replaced by the seemingly direct contact and apparent immediacy of paint tube to surface. To come any closer is to enter directly into the category of the real, which is precisely what happens with the response to the air as fresh and cold.

> Up closer, a wild iris, white and yellow,
> fresh-squiggled from the tube.
> The air is fresh and cold; cold early spring
> clear as gray glass; a half inch of blue sky
> below the steel-gray storm clouds.
> (They were the artist's specialty.)
> A specklike bird is flying to the left.
> Or is it a flyspeck looking like a bird? (*CP*, 176)

The seeming tangibility and vividness of objects increases with their proximity. At least, this is how Bishop's poem proceeds, guided by the optical logic of the painting. It is similar to the way in which vivid effects of seemingly tangible objects are produced in the stereoscope.[31] Crary documents how pronounced stereoscopic effects depend upon the presence of objects or obtrusive forms in the near or middle ground; there must be enough points in the image that require significant changes in the angle of convergence of the optical axes to produce the impression of three-dimensional solidity.

A singular "wild iris" is the closest thing that "Poem" gives us to obstruct the smooth passage to a vanishing point in the distance. The iris seems to be most real when named as if outside the representational space, shed of the modifiers "tiny" or "miniature." It appears to elude the grasp of representation—a real flower visibly drawn near—even as it flips readily into squiggles of white and yellow paint. The repetition of "fresh" points to the sensation that accompanies the direct, though mismatched, collusion of representation and object. Not only the object, but the medium itself, feels fresh and tangible.

Paradoxically, the effect of tangibility results, in optically enhanced vision, from the failure of vision to encompass the other senses. Tangibility is peculiarly detached from something we can touch, existing only as the experience of the limitations of visual process. The stereoscope in particular calls attention to vision as a medium for concentrating all the senses.[32] The meta-dimension which the stereoscope introduces is the visual experience of sense. The challenge this optic poses to a writer such as Bishop is not that of describing an image or referent, but of describing sensory experience as *seeing*. When we think we can touch a visual abstraction (as in the stereoscope) or a quasi-visual concrete detail ("Poem"), we experience two sensations: vision as a tangible effect, and touch as visually abstracted. The fact that we experience, in a poem, neither touch nor vision, nor indeed any of the five senses except with respect to the book or page at hand, does not diminish the capacity of the poet to articulate historical shifts between the senses. It may enhance it by concentrating the problem, common to all sign systems, into a discursive one: we lack a discourse for primary sense, and historically, a way to describe new acts of seeing. How do we sense sense, or, how do we sense seeing? Bishop would perform it, through language acts.

The obvious literary analogue for stereoscopic realism is synaesthesia. The experience of the disjunctions between the senses—through the attempt to describe one sense in terms of another—intensifies the reality of these effects. The intersense analogy brings to the fore the differences between the senses, as when touch is described in visual terms. A heightened awareness is produced, which might be called unity or the real, but which seems to derive from the fact that the interstices between the senses, whether disjunctions or contiguities, are knowable only physiologically. Synaesthesia foregrounds sensory indeterminacy; the subject can only know the interstices between the senses as a physiological process. Thus to name or *write* these interstices is to ask that the reader read physiologically. This is Bishop's operative illusion: in producing the effect of a real image, to the point that we can seem to touch it, she invites us to experience the verbal discrepancy between sight and touch as a physiological one.

In "Poem," back in the distance, stereoscopic uncertainty is produced through chiasmus: the question of identifying what something looks like points to the indeterminacy of two looks conjoined in one: "A specklike bird is flying to the left. / Or is it a flyspeck looking like a bird?" "Like" is doubled upon "like," "speck" on "speck," "fly" on "fly," and "bird" on "bird," each with a different inflection through the exchanged word order, and underscored by the extra, more minute chiasmus of "speck*li* . . ." and ". . . *ly*speck." In the effort to ask what it looks like, only "looking" emerges singularly through the repetitions. In chiasmus, that question crosses irresolvably with the question of what to name it. The visual and verbal poles cross in chiasma—by anatomical definition, an intersection, especially of the optic nerves. In Bishop's "Crusoe in England," the "unrenameable" island of Crusoe is contrasted to a volcanic island seen from a ship: "a black fleck—basalt, probably— / rose in the mate's binoculars / and caught on the horizon like a fly" (*CP*, 162). Here the aid of binoculars likewise focuses at the intersection of optical recognition and the effort to name. The slippage between "fly" and "fleck" is minute, almost too small to merit mention. Yet Bishop does mention it, with a notable similarity of attention in these two poems, enough to highlight the significance for this poet of the intersection, the "fleck," between optical and linguistic indeterminacy: the visual-verbal chiasmus of "specklike" and "flyspeck" produces "fleck."

"Poem," as will "The Fish," passes into a second, less literal phase of seeing: recognition. The same visual details, re-seen from a slightly different point of view, open onto a past history. Unlike the flesh-to-flesh encounter with the otherness of a natural thing in "The Fish," however, here the poet-observer is gathered into a shared artistic, and therefore domestic, vision of a place she knew as a child. "It" becomes a jubilant signifier of a shared reference point.

> Heavens, I recognize the place, I know it!
> It's behind—I can almost remember the farmer's name.
> His barn backed on that meadow. There it is,
> titanium white, one dab. The hint of steeple,
> filaments of brush-hairs, barely there,
> must be the Presbyterian church.
> Would that be Miss Gillespie's house?
> Those particular geese and cows
> are naturally before my time. (*CP*, 176–177)

The various points of intersection between her memory of the place and what she is presently seeing are important as sites of slippage and uncertainty. The pleasure of this painting is that its miniature size requires the observer to look for, and in so doing recognize, the real barn, house, geese and cows, through the little dabs of paint, thus producing a slightly-off, stereoscopic version of visual accuracy. Bishop's untiring efforts to make visible description seem actually to work are stereoscopic, rather than microscopic, insofar as they structurally acknowledge failure through images, not of generic things, but of painted, doubled, and particular, "geese." Equal descriptive detail is granted to the signifier ("titanium white," "filaments of brush-hairs") and the referent ("the Presbyterian church," "Miss Gillespie's house"), enhancing the reality effect of each. Recognition is aligned with the signified; the success of the effort to locate the precise "there" is, paradoxically, also the failure of the conflation of the artificial medium with the natural place it depicts. The apparatus instantaneously re-separates from the view at this point of "recognition" of both the place and the poem/painting's representational failure. The irony of the phrase "naturally before my time," given the poem's penchant for ephemeral natural things such as flowers, geese and cows, and "yet-to-be-dismantled elms," is that this painting's naturalism is achieved through the artificial stilling of time. "As if there were an instrument like a telescope or microscope—for time—" writes Bishop about a Piero della Francesca painting, "you're looking straight through dark centuries into bright sunlight, only it's all silent—."[33]

Bishop is less interested in "Poem" in the differences of time, history, place and point of view than in their faulty convergence, through modern-day time travel, into a half-commercial, half-domestic image currency. To achieve the desired visibility effect, Bishop emphasizes distinctly verbal slippages in unified perspective, drawn from the poetic tradition, through puns, repetition, chiasmus, and other tropes. That the sketch is done "in one breath" draws attention to how the poet and the painter never share the same breath. Only in the illusion that the "air is fresh and cold" is this possible.

> A sketch done in an hour, "in one breath,"
> once taken from a trunk and handed over.
> *Would you like this? I'll probably never*
> *have room to hang these things again.*
> *Your Uncle George, no, mine, my Uncle George,*
> *he'd be your great-uncle, left them all with Mother*
> *when he went back to England.*
> *You know, he was quite famous, an R.A. . . . . (CP, 177)*

The interspersion of a relative's voice—a "literal" quote which details the familial relation and biographical facts of the painter—likewise sets off how the real voice is heard through a three-dimensional silence; between the loudness of the quoted voice, and the relative silence of the painting, the poem creates the effect of Bishop's real voice. Bishop enacts here, as in "The Moose" or "In the Waiting Room," a verbal reality of the poet's presence—an effect that is akin to that of O'Hara's.

> I never knew him. We both knew this place,
> apparently, this literal small backwater,
> looked at it long enough to memorize it,
> our years apart. How strange. And it's still loved,
> or its memory is (it must have changed a lot). (CP, 177)

Pointing to the impossible gaps between them—"I never knew him," "our years apart," "(it must have changed a lot)"—Bishops polarizes the differences in order to create the third dimension in which they do meet. A version of Simmel's modern interpersonal exchange, in which face-to-face communication is navigated through the eyes,[34] here it is the poet's words that enable an intersection of eyes. What follows is Bishop's unusually explicit account of the poetic effort she has been engaged in all along: to coincide, to compress, to cramp—each finally imprecise because the very slippage between our different words for things is the point to which she draws our attention. By emending "visions" to "looks," and thereby admitting to the flaws of her own language, as well as alerting us to her peculiar philosophy (no "vision" without literal looking), Bishop would have us understand the failure of figurative language as a poetic opportunity. "Visions" assumes that we can be launched flawlessly into art; "looks" are more "live," and "touching in detail" because they are aware of their limitations.

> Our visions coincided—"visions" is
> too serious a word—our looks, two looks:
> art "copying from life" and life itself,
> life and the memory of it so compressed
> they've turned into each other. Which is which?
> Life and the memory of it cramped,
> dim, on a piece of Bristol board,
> dim, but how live, how touching in detail
> —the little that we get for free,
> the little of our earthly trust. Not much.
> About the size of our abidance
> along with theirs: the munching cows,
> the iris, crisp and shivering, the water
> still standing from spring freshets,
> the yet-to-be-dismantled elms, the geese. (CP, 177)

The last lines of the poem enter into the most sustained illusion available to the poetic "look" that knows its own flaws. The effect is one of words exactly aligned with their referents, in which the readerly experience of the signified is suspended at the point of semiotic collapse. The tenuous tangibility of the iris "crisp and shivering," the seeming disregard of the "munching cows," and the "yet-to-be-dismantled elms," seem to reach out beyond their verbal construction as if to be actually visible, palpable, "touching in detail." Bishop's placement of quotations in the poem— " 'visions' " and "art 'copying from life' "—calls attention to the inadequacy of terminology, and the over-seriousness of what Burke calls "abstract compound words," in the service of poetry (or poetic criticism, where these terms frequently appear). Language is obscure, "dim," but by narrowing it to words that seem to correspond to pictures and concrete details, Bishop makes it into an illuminant.

Poetry, as Bishop would have it, is no more dim than the uncle's painting with its actual colors and representations of animals and landscape. Awareness of the flaws of both linguistic and optical apparatuses slips away precisely where the two apparatuses seem to converge. Two looks, or rather, one shared look through a stereoscopic apparatus, produces an extra view—not much, "literal, small," yet one that belongs to the reader too. The meaningfulness (in semiotic terms, the signified) is a function of how little there is. The more literal and fixed on minute, verbal details, the smaller the corresponding focus of the visual apparatus. Yet the deeper the proportion of meaning, and the larger the sensation of the reality effect.

MAGNIFYING LENS

Emily Dickinson wittily mentions microscopes as "prudent In an Emergency"[35]— a converse to the fine invention for seeing by "Faith," when faith fails. Bishop's microscopic magnifying acts do work as a kind of faith, as her daring acts of magnification seem based on a sense of necessity. The effort is not merely to illuminate what the eyes normally see, but to make visible what cannot be seen, in order to keep something else at bay. Her optics come in varied and multiple forms, including animal eyes, water droplets, miniatures, boxes, paintings; of the technical instruments, the camera obscura and stereoscope among them, many are specifically instruments of magnification: the microscope, telescope, magnifying glass, and binoculars. These latter instruments especially share the common feature of constraining the act of seeing to its intensification. Each offers a release from the strain of seeing too much (and vicariously, of thinking too self-consciously) through the self-forgetful pleasure in "small things" seen close-up.[36]

Mary McCarthy observes how Bishop enters into a paradox of proportions. She speaks to the personal costs as well as the aesthetic value of Bishop's art of magnification: "I would like to have had her quiddity, her way of seeing that was like a big pocket magnifying glass. Of course it would have hurt to use it for ordinary looking: that would have been the forfeit."[37] The release into the poetic vastness of small spaces may inversely, in the world's enlarged spaces, generate the feeling of being disproportionately small and peripheral. The fable of the Giant Toad in "Rainy Season; Sub-Tropics" addresses the painful sense of disproportion in this structural chiasmus: "My eyes bulge and hurt. They are my one great beauty even so. They see too much, above, below, and yet there is not much to see" (*CP*, 139). The fable explores from the inside out the problem of being all eye, where seeing exposes as much it protects, and being oversize in one way renders one as vulnerable and small as a snail or a toad in others.

To read as if with a magnifying glass is how Bishop describes reading the poems of her friend and contemporary, Robert Lowell. Her blurb for the book-jacket of Lowell's *Life Studies* (1959) reads as follows:

> As a child, I used to look at my grandfather's Bible under a powerful reading-glass. The letters assembled beneath the lens were suddenly like a Lowell poem, as big as life and as alive, and rainbow-edged. It seemed to illuminate as it magnified; it could also be used as a burning-glass.[38]

Where the description reads "a Lowell poem," we readily see by metonymy that this is "a Bishop poem." Bishop aspires to a prismatic literalism in which verbal experience is seen, and has visual effects in excess of the mere content of reading. What is described is not the content, but the category of reading, exclusively accessed by gazing through this optic. On those occasions when Bishop takes literalism as far as seeing the letters of a poem, she does not push it as far as Stevens does to exclude the impression of also seeing real images. In this example, as in the reading of "The Fish" that follows, the vision of a poem and its letters as "rainbow-edged" is spiritual in a way that does not derive from themes or content. Displaced from, as well as connected to, the patriarchal and religious traditions that would inscribe the optic as grandfather's, or the book as the Bible, the experience of the reading-glass is an access to the phenomenon of reading: Bishop's rainbow denotes the positive, prismatic, binocular experience of the slippages between seeing and reading.

In her celebrated poem of 1940, "The Fish," Bishop converts the poetic exercise of still-life description into a phenomenal exercise in seeing a natural, non-intentional being close-up. The reader's eye is magnified to a point of seeming to see too much, such that the sensation of excessive seeing becomes its own experience. Frequently anthologized and praised as a poem of objective visual description, "The Fish" has been read (and effectively, *seen*) many times, with ever more minute attention. The literal referent for the poem is a Caribbean jewfish Bishop caught in 1938 in Key West.[39] Not only does the poem detail with minute attention the visible exterior of the fish, it renders visible through simile and imaginative visualization the fish's concealed interior. It explores bipolar relations—notably between seeing and saying—precisely at the point at which it makes a claim on microscopic accuracy.

> Here and there
> his brown skin hung in strips
> like ancient wallpaper,
> and its pattern of darker brown
> was like wallpaper:
> shapes like full-blown roses
> stained and lost through age.   (*CP*, 42)

The eye begins to focus on a visible surface: the skin of the fish, half stripping off, invites further investigation of its fleshy border. Advancing by simile, Bishop links the literal fish exterior ("strips," "pattern," and "shapes") and the lining of a domestic interior. Overlapping and in parallel with each other, the two surfaces tenuously converge to create the effect of three-dimensionality. Neither paper nor skin is actually present before the eye, but each seems to take on a materiality through the collapse of the simile. In the overlapping patterns of fish skin and wallpaper, the "elsewhere" of a dimly recollected domesticity is borrowed as a lens through which to see the tangible "here" of vivid shapes "like full-blown roses." As the third in a line of similes, "shapes like full-blown roses" creates a vivid reality effect precisely where it refers both to the wallpaper and the fish. The inadequacy of language to enact double vision is compensated for by the senses, and in particular, by vision. The claim that we see the "skin" of the fish combines with an awareness of these similes on "paper" to produce an effect of a visible real.

Anne Stevenson notes Bishop's capacity to describe two or more things at once—like fish skin and wallpaper—as an instance of a poet's advantage over a painter. She observes Bishop's command of metaphor to be "sophisticated but accurate."[40] Her assumption that tropes of comparison advance the cause of accuracy is significant, as is the suggestion that the poet exceeds the painter in accuracy by access to multiple (albeit metaphoric) visual scenes. The eye is Bishop's privileged measure of the real, and she takes tropes of vision to be the closest possible approximation to the real eye in poetry. It is curious that among tropic possibilities, therefore, Bishop frequently opts in "The Fish" for similes over metaphors, which draw attention to the artifice of the linkage rather than elide it. The ripple of "likes" in three of four lines—"like ancient wallpaper," "like wallpaper," "like full-blown roses"—underscores the linguistic process that generates vivid effects. Verbal directives to see imaginary objects, Scarry has argued, enhance their vividness because they suggest something is there for the taking.[41] A back-and-forth between verbal directives and imagery does enhance the reality effects of "The Fish"; it also perplexes whether the relation between seeing and saying is one of complementarity or substitution. If one sees the "fish," is it merely the subject of the poem, or does it come to speak for the poem? Does the "eye" of the fish complement or substitute for the "I" of the poem, or does it substitute *as* the poem? Bishop multiplies the directives as to what the fish is "like," compounding a sense that there is indeed an actual fish, while increasing the ambiguity in the relation between the verbal and the visual.

As the eye zooms closer in, Bishop attempts to generate an image so minutely detailed as to be incontrovertible as fact. In this case the figure of objective visibility—at once the lens and the thing seen—is the body of the fish. Any subjective impressions cling and burrow into the apparent skin of the object: "speckled with barnacles," "rosettes of lime" and "tiny white sea-lice." From skin, or paper/surface, we enter a 3-D illusion of skin and flesh. This effect of seeing obscures any other focus; whatever we know of the unseen narrator is concealed in the "accurate" detailing of the fish.

> He was speckled with barnacles,
> fine rosettes of lime,
> and infested
> with tiny white sea-lice (*CP*, 42)

A predilection for the small, the ornamental, and what Thomas Travisano refers to as the "indelicate detail,"[42] challenges the subject to look closely, perhaps even dangerously close. A way of seeing that relies upon words is concealed within but also potentially effaced by the visible "reality" of the fish. Rather than safely hiding the human observer—the promise of the camera obscura—a danger emerges in this model of the magnified eye that the enlarged, multi-faceted fish will so capture our visual attention as to absorb us altogether. Bishop's gift, particularly in "The Fish," is to school our eye's minutest directions in physically reading; this exercise makes a potentially aggressive or coercive demand upon the reader to *see*. A simple mimesis of "art 'copying from life,'" in which words are the seemingly transparent conduits of images, is turned into a supermimesis of over-transparency.

This danger of seeing too much, too clearly, also rebounds upon the poet-narrator. Minor indelicacies evolve into a more sinister meditation on the gills of fish, which vacillate between opening and closing. Though she holds the fish "half out of water," what remains unspoken is that the fish holds her figuratively half in the water. The speculation on the fish's perspective—that he fears the "terrible oxygen"—flips over to her own fear of the "frightening gills":

> While his gills were breathing in
> the terrible oxygen—
> the frightening gills,
> fresh and crisp with blood . . . (*CP*, 42)

Entering too far into the psychology of the fish exposes her to the dangerous exteriority of the gills, and further, to the fear of being trapped out of her element, unable to breathe. The point of exchange between the fish, who feels the oxygen to be "terrible," and the subject, who feels the gills to be "frightening," is syntactically underemphasized: terrible and frightening seem to be two parts of the same experience. Marilyn May Lombardi observes that this passage is preinscribed by Bishop's own connection, as an asthmatic, between terror and the loss of oxygen.[43] Predictably, Bishop retreats into the safety of visual literalism; removing herself from narrative danger, she dares instead an entrance into the flesh of the fish through the magnified eye. With the shift "While his gills . . . // . . . I thought," she introduces temporal meta-dimensionality so visually particulate as potentially to substitute for rather than merely complement the first account. The passage into the fish interior leads with the misnomer, "I thought," even as whatever thinking follows is sensorily particulate, and abstract only insofar as it is synaesthetic—a seeming visibility of the tangible. Sensory rather than cognitive, "thought" is concentrated into the magnified eye; this "optic" sees more than the normal eye, paradoxically, by way of the same verbal directives it ignores. Bishop achieves her daring, scopic entrance into the "coarse white flesh"—impossible insofar as one cannot see the interior flesh of a "live" fish—without a blink in credibility. Imaginative crossover, the trope of chiasmus, is only risked at the level of the verbally magnified eye:

> I thought of the coarse white flesh
> packed in like feathers,
> the big bones and the little bones,
> the dramatic reds and blacks
> of his shiny entrails,
> and the pink swim-bladder
> like a big peony. (CP, 42)

Bishop borrows from the scientific capacity to see more through a magnifying, and even x-ray, lens than the naked eye can see alone. The "shiny entrails" are not transcendent images, with manifest meaning, but scientifically accurate organs of the fish interior. The similes connect an exterior sphere of actual feathers and flowers to an interior one of flesh and organs. One can no more see from outside a nondisembodied fish a "pink swim-bladder" than "a big peony," but as before, the trope of visual comparison acts like a two-eyed magnifying apparatus, whereby one thing seems more materially particulate, and therefore "real," through the lens of the other.

The dramatic locus of encounter for visual comparison is of course the eyes of the fish. The lens of the other, if it does not reciprocate one's gaze, may intensify the capacity to see oneself as real. That Bishop's narrator seeks to know the fish through one privileged channel—the visual sense— is a clue that she locates the key to her own self-knowledge in the eyes.

> I looked into his eyes
> which were far larger than mine
> but shallower, and yellowed,
> the irises backed and packed
> with tarnished tinfoil
> seen through the lenses
> of old scratched isinglass. (CP, 42–43)

By giving a close-up description of another's eyes, Bishop reveals to us something about her own. Her "I" is inscribed into his "eyes": the multiple instances of "I" and variations of "is" and "in" embedded into such words as "irises," "tinfoil" and "isinglass" are instances of how she writes herself into the act of seeing. Within the shallow anatomy of the mere "irises" is a deep emotional concentration. The near repetition within the phrase "backed and packed," compounded with the earlier "packed" fish flesh, suggests how Bishop's gesture is one of reinforcing and concentrating through the increasingly metaphoric attention to the fish. The very form of the poem supports this; each detail is backed by another in a series of short, compact lines.

A shallow view of the visible world, bound as if with a scientist's perimeters, allows for safety in concealment. But within this shallowness resides a highly sensitive perspective, itself with a whole depth of personal history that is variously tarnished, old, scratched. Bishop departs from poetic tradition by dangling from her lines an old male fish that promises not the "unseen," but magnified visibility.[44] What this enhanced visibility is for, what its purpose is, is the conundrum Bishop trains her optic not to see. Its focus hides nothing less than the viewer herself. The fact that the "lenses" seen through belong to the fish, and further are of "isinglass" (gelatin composed from fish air-bladders) points to how she would not claim the lenses as her own. By comparative size and emotional weight, her eyes are therefore smaller than what she sees. The fish has all the poem's adjectives of size—"tremendous," "big," "larger"—on its side, while the poet-observer, who is never once herself described, occupies the "little rented boat."[45] Size, weight, and optical perspective become the literal markers of a sense of smallness that is far more subjective than Bishop would let on.

Exploring the literal sites of entrance into the fish interior, Bishop moves from the gills and eyes to the privileged orifice of the poem: the fish's mouth. The connective link between poet and fish is introduced in the opening lines, "my hook / fast in a corner of his mouth," where her lines catch and speak for the fish from a peripheral hook. We learn in the opening that the fish "hung a grunting weight," the modifier referring to the short, guttural sound some fish make when out of water. But the closest approximation to words, from the mouth of the fish, are the visible signifiers that hang from its mouth: "the five big hooks / grown firmly in his mouth."

> I admired his sullen face,
> the mechanism of his jaw,
> and then I saw
> that from his lower lip
> —if you could call it a lip—
> grim, wet, and weaponlike,
> hung five old pieces of fish-line,
> or four and a wire leader
> with the swivel still attached,
> with all their five big hooks
> grown firmly in his mouth.
> A green line, frayed at the end
> where he broke it, two heavier lines,
> and a fine black thread
> still crimped from the strain and snap

> when it broke and he got away.
> Like medals with their ribbons
> frayed and wavering,
> a five-haired beard of wisdom
> trailing from his aching jaw. (*CP*, 43)

A chasm and chiasm opens up between seeing for the first time and the recognition of the past history and otherness of the fish. What was overlooked in the initial hooking of the fish mouth is now seen and comprehended. The mouth that says in the opening lines "He didn't fight. / He hadn't fought at all" is supplanted by the eyes that perceive "grim, wet, and weaponlike / . . . five old pieces of fish-line." Insight (or history) is achieved where the mouth of the poet speaks as if through an optic, where seeing the lip of the fish prompts the question of "—if [whether] you could call it a lip—," and the slippery visible referents of words make a chiastic claim on cognition. The slippage between seeing, counting, and saying is paradoxically at once concealed and magnified by this very careful form of lip-reading. Bishop's attention to the color, shape and material of each line and hook, and the impulse to emend and self-correct the visible facts actually intensifies the strain upon poetic language to see clearly, reliably and mimetically. Is it four lines, or five? The effort to see "five old pieces of fish line, / or four and a wire leader" is not resolved by the counting and renaming that follows. The relation of "or" sets up an inexact exchange between "five big hooks," "green line . . . / . . .two heavier lines, / and a fine black thread," and/or "five-haired beard." Bishop has us literally seeing/reading between the lines.

Precisely where the strain of dualism is recognized as a snap, and one that has occurred repeatedly, is where we are suspended in a third place—between what has happened and what will happen: ". . . a fine black thread / still crimped from the strain and snap / when it broke and he got away." He will get away, but has not yet, and the only line not visibly described—but readably inscribed—is the one from which he now hangs. This invisible line, with meanings that cannot be seen, is concealed within the visible lines. The multiple definitions of the word "crimp" alone show how much is concentrated into the visible lines: to fold; to entrap; to gash (as of the flesh of a fish). We can all but see the fundamental flaw of figurative language. To the extent that we do "see" it, it is in the form of a severed black thread—a single poetic line, or vertically dangled, "The Fish," a long and conspicuously short-lined poem.

Here it is worth reiterating Jarraway's claim that "paradoxically, the purest gauge of what ideally cannot be seen (or seen readily) is what 'the real eye,' in fact, does see and perhaps sees only too well. . . ."[46] The fish is the principal source of visibility in the poem, and also what can least be known. To sustain a victory, to reach a form of knowing—since Bishop does not cast her own blind spots as blind—is to see through an intensified

optic. With the phrase "I stared and stared," the figurative act of seeing
stalls, and the abundance of visual reference spills over into a description
of the vehicle of the poem itself. The context from which the "I/eye"
speaks—the poem—is here seen as the mechanism of engine, boat, and oil.

> I stared and stared
> and victory filled up
> the little rented boat,
> from the pool of bilge
> where oil had spread a rainbow
> around the rusted engine
> to the bailer rusted orange,
> the sun-cracked thwarts,
> the oarlocks on their strings,
> the gunnels—until everything
> was rainbow, rainbow, rainbow!
> And I let the fish go. (*CP*, 143–144)

Oil, as the medium that spreads this rainbow vision, is a distinctly modern
and industrial substance, below the eyes (in an essential inversion of heav-
enly sight) rather than above. The syllabic repetition of "oil" in "Filling
Station" circulates the baseline textual fluid as an everyday man's
covenant: a "fill up," as at a modern-day station of the cross. And this is
significant given the Biblical origins of the rainbow as a sign of the
covenant, seen by Noah after the floods, overhead in a cloud. Bishop's look
downward at the oil, and the literal engine that in its suspension powers
the poem, inverts Biblical, upward vision in the clouds. Bishop's sighting,
and multiple citings, of "rainbow," are those of literal seeing: word sightings through the prism of language, like the rainbow-edged letters of a
Lowell poem, or the magnified letters of her Grandfather's Bible.

This is not exactly a grounded vision either, but more like her at once literal and liminal Key West harbor, a "houseboat" for herself or Stevens,
"out in a small inboard motorboat, fishing in the evening." A little rented
boat and a two-eyed fish in lieu of Noah's ark, and a pool of dirty bilge
water filling it up for a flood, are enough to produce a flesh-to-flesh, eye-
to-eye encounter that opens out onto the sublimity of rainbow. In the
phrase "sun-cracked thwarts" is the idea of light passing through what
frustrates or blocks it. Bishop responds to what "thwarts" figurative seeing
by forcing visual tropes beyond the point of breaking. Where figurative
language attempts to catch the referent, casting its lines from the five
senses—and they break—a further line is let out. The fabled sixth sense.

The extra-sensory moment, the sensation of the signified slipping back in—
intensified by the repetition of "rainbow, rainbow, rainbow!"—is achieved
when the staging of figurative failure is recognized as a false stage. For in fact

there is a victory, ascribed neither to the fish nor to the "eye/I," but that seems to belong to the poem. Victory does not anchor, or drown, the little boat, but fills it up. Precisely where the vehicle for seeing so intently and minutely would sink under its own weight, it instead empties itself out into the doubled, vacant fixation of the eye: "I stared and stared." And this blank staring—in which sight partially detaches from the visible referent it is fixed on—creates a vacancy for language, or the partial awareness of it, to fill up the blank.

Seeing the broken lines that dangle from the fish mouth enables a positive recognition of victory—the knowledge of the poem slipping back in. The singular form of "a rainbow" is exchanged for the multiplicity of "rainbow, rainbow, rainbow!" In a triple repetition, by which the word is released from its subordinate status to the referent, rainbow is simultaneously seen and read, as real image and pure word, in a three-dimensional effect of a binocular structure. The poem's final admission of severance, of letting go of what has always already let go—the line between the literal and the figurative—is registered as a positive experience. The failure of sense, and of the privileged sense—vision—in poetry, is converted into a prismatic effect of the real, and of the really read.

REALITY EFFECT

> The books
> I'd read were full of blanks;
> the poems—well, I tried
> reciting to my iris-beds,
> "They flash upon that inward eye,
> which is the bliss . . ." The bliss of what? (*CP*, 164)

The detail of the iris-beds in Bishop's long, late autobiographical poem, "Crusoe in England" (1971), marks a crucial conjoining of the two versions of irises we have encountered thus far, as a doubled, wild-painted flower in "Poem," and as an anatomical component of the eyes in "The Fish." There is a third, etymological version, deriving from Greek mythology, that of Iris, the goddess of the rainbow. In this excerpt from "Crusoe," Bishop offers a sensation of looking at a real image—always filtered for her, as we have explored, through prismatic, rainbow-edged letters. In this case, the poem's visual structure (following the anatomical irises) is mirrored by the narrative content (the floral iris), to produce what should be a third, multi-colored visibility effect (the rainbow). Bishop sets this up, instead, as an anti-climatic experience of drawing a blank—a kind of writer's block that occurs while seeing something. Bishop's identification with Robinson Crusoe, to the point of over-identification, is complex,[47] but here it suffices to note that Crusoe was to have ship-wrecked on an island north of Brazil on his way back to England—an unlikely place for irises to grow, but a likely point of identification for Bishop, writing the poem in

New England, after having spent an unusually happy and productive stretch of her life in Brazil.

To recite to one's iris-beds (the narrator recalls this), is to resight and re-site them in the absence of a book. This is perfect for Bishop: seeing one's own eyes projected into the material flora of an exterior world acts as an allegory for an absent reading/writing—an absence that then returns, in the act of reading, as an effect of the visible real. But what was perfect, on an island (eye-land), is now drearily retold as a filled-in blank, for back at home the anachronistically missing word of Wordsworth's "I Wandered Lonely As a Cloud" (which Defoe's Crusoe could not possibly have read) is readily resupplied; Bishop's Crusoe tells us "One of the first things that I did / when I got back was look that up":

> For oft, when on my couch I lie
> In vacant or in pensive mood,
> They flash upon that inward eye
> Which is the bliss of *solitude*;
> And then my heart with pleasure fills,
> And dances with the daffodils. (Lines 13–18)

Wordsworth's inner-eye vision contrasts with Bishop's outer-eye seeing; significantly, she chooses the convergence of their two passages (or, two perspectives mismatched via anachronism) to stage the differences in their dual seeing. Where Wordsworth's "I" lies on a literal couch, in a vacant or pensive mood, receiving the recollected image of daffodils, Bishop's "I" stares directly at the literal "iris-beds," and is unable to recollect a single (and to that extent, solitary) word, in the absence of its context in a poem in a book. Nothing fills the blank or vacancy, for it is already filled with the irises, with a pun on "I's" and "eyes." Instead of seizing the moment to generate her prismatic binocularity, Bishop casts this as an instance of aphasia. The displacement between the vividly recollected daffodils and the overly-visible irises hinges upon a missing word (solitude), which to Bishop, as a compound abstract word, is alarmingly lacking in a visible ref-erent. Her blind spot is the abstract category of articulation, exemplified by "solitude," that cannot, in effect, be seen. In order for this spot in Wordsworth's poem, embedded within Bishop's iris-beds, to be refilled, the reader must supply it, "look it up." The brilliant effect, announced to be missing, is supplied by the absence/presence of a reader.

In "The Reality Effect," Barthes offers a theory as to why a concrete detail such as "iris-beds" would be extra-invested with meaning. It also works as a theory as to why the missing "solitude" would be placed in the periphery or blank spots of a text.[48] In Barthes' theory of the superfluous detail, built from an account of French realism, he claims that a set of details in Flaubert's description of Madame Aubain's room in *Un Coeur*

Simple does not advance the narrative toward a specific end: "on an old piano, under a barometer, there was a pyramid of boxes."[49] The inessential, disposable character of details grows out of a major shift in aesthetics, according to Barthes. Whereas Western culture has traditionally ascribed the end of such details to beauty (granting an aesthetic function to ekphrasis and other narratively dispensable instances of description), modern imperatives force the question of function, requiring a justification for the aesthetic detail. He argues that peripheral textual details such as the "barometer" mark the collapse of two heretofore discrete discourses: the "vraisemblable" (imitation or poetry) and the "real" (history). The resulting discourse, which Barthes calls, to cite one among his shifting set of terms, the "new vraisemblance," consists of statements whose only justification is their referent. "Obsessive reference to the 'concrete,'" he writes, "is always brandished as a weapon against meaning, as if there were some indisputable law that what is truly alive could not signify." The concrete detail acts as the reality that carries no further meaning. Barthes concludes: "Flaubert's barometer, Michelet's little door, say, in the last analysis, only this: we are the real."[50]

Barthes embeds an interesting invitation to interdisciplinary methods in his essay; his large claim that the detail marks the convergence of historical and literary discourse is followed up by the more particular point that the development of literary techniques to authenticate the real is roughly contemporaneous with historical developments such as photography and reportage. Martin Jay advances this connection by comparing Barthes' theory of "the reality effect" (1968) with that of the earlier "photographic paradox" (1961).[51] Central to each theory is the semiotic structure of pure denotation: a direct encounter of referent and signifier. Barthes argues in "The Photographic Message" that the power of the photographic medium to generate analogons to reality is strong enough to impress upon a viewer the experience of a pure encounter between the object and its simulacrum; "in front of a photograph, the feeling of 'denotation', or, if one prefers, analogical plenitude, is so great that the description of a photograph is literally impossible."[52] Photographs as such (here he means the limited sense of press photos) send the same message as Flaubert's details: we are the real.

Aphasia is set off by the feeling of denotation, not simply denotation itself. Barthes is describing, in structuralist terms, the experience of not being able to describe. To isolate the detail, as Barthes does, is to precipitate not only the question of seeing the detail, but of seeing the reading of the detail. For no detail can be extricated from this polar structure of seeing and reading. Barthes describes the logic in semiotic terms:

> Semiotically, the 'concrete detail' is constituted by the direct collusion of a referent and a signifier . . . This is what might be called the referential illusion. The truth behind this illusion is this: eliminated from the realist

utterance as a signified of denotation, the 'real' slips back in as a signified
of connotation; for at the very moment when these details are supposed to
denote reality directly, all that they do, tacitly, is signify it . . . It is the category of the 'real' and not its various contents, which is being signified.[53]

The illusion that we are seeing something actually provokes an experience
of the failure of denotative process. Thus in Bishop's "iris" or Barthes'
"barometer" (the latter an instrument for measuring atmospheric pressure,
the former a bed for the pupil that measures amounts of light), details are
pressurized with extra-function to signify the category (not any concrete
content) of the real. The tinier the detail, the more pressurized it becomes,
and the more it wants to flip into the category of the real. In the example
of "Poem" ("up closer, a wild iris, white and yellow, / fresh-squiggled from
the tube"), the effort to make the iris wild, visible in its natural state, back-
fires; what is signified is the category of the real image as its own sensation.
But the new *vraisemblance* of Barthes' definition has two poles: visual reality and linguistic irreality. And of course Bishop's does too, but the pole of
linguistic irreality is extremely hard to see (or rather, one cannot but read
it) because the effects of visual reality are so pronounced in her work.

Absolute verbal denotation, as Stevens attempts, blocks a certain kind of
seeing; absolute visual denotation, which Bishop aspires to, restricts certain
kinds of verbalization. One can only describe what is visually before the
eyes; one can say "iris-beds," ("I is" embedded in it), but not "solitude."
Schor's summary of Barthes clarifies how language works as an optic,
deriving out of the failure of realism:

> What falsifies realism from the very start is the fact that our vision of the
> real is refracted through the prism of language; there exists no relationship
> to the real which is not mediated through the opaque medium of language.[54]

Bishop's strategy of abundant referentiality does not substantiate the real,
but generates a new real: the supplemental effects of a linguistic, rather
than mimetic, realism. As such, this new real is the product of a conflation
of discourses. Where Stevens makes the point of this new real more
emphatically and exclusively for the poetic medium, through a self-
conscious negation of the referential illusion, Bishop draws poetry into a
shared discourse, most especially with optics, by abundantly satisfying the
illusion. Her critique that Stevens' poetry should "have more unconscious
spots left in,"[55] is a clue to the necessity of her own blind spot. If one looks
too closely at language, it ceases to be an optic, and one loses the pleasure
of seeing. Far from debunking the referential illusion, Bishop partially mys-
tifies it, but always in a way that registers the problem of verbal representation *within* the visual scene.

Bishop's investment in the trivial detail does not proliferate to the
extreme it will in a later generation of American poetry, amply evidenced
in O'Hara's work. Her embrace of the literal belies her experimentalism.
The literal trap of visual details is also Bishop's trick, for she locates them

not at the margins of narrative, like Barthes' examples from French realism, but as the magnified center of her poetic discourse. Her model is organic in a way that Barthes resists, for it emphasizes that we re-see details not as peripheral to texts, but as their vital component. Mobilizing contradictions, as between necessity and uselessness, reality and the aesthetic, readability and visibility, she generates a prismatic convergence via the steps, leaps and inversions of their binocularity.

CHAPTER III

Cinematic Effects: Frank O'Hara

NOT A PAINTER

In his monograph on Jackson Pollock, Frank O'Hara admiringly describes *"Number 12, 1952"*:

> . . . it is a big, brassy gigolo of a painting; for the first time the aluminum paint looks like money, and the color is that of the sunset in a technicolor Western. But its peculiar quality is its natural vulgarity: it is not beautiful, but it *is* real."[1]

O'Hara stages an aesthetic, not of beauty, but of the real, through his reading/writing of Pollock's painting. He resolves the tension between what the painting is like, and what it "is," only at the far end of rhetorical excess and slippage, at the fifth instance of "is": "it *is* real." O'Hara generates a word-currency of artistic-commercial hybrids through which the real is posited. Words associated with traditional aesthetics—"paint," "color," "natural," and "beautiful"—cross in oxymoron with words often associated with tastelessness and the depreciation of aesthetic values such as "money," "technicolor," "gigolo," and "vulgarity." And the inconsistency of these word pairings both at the level of structure (metaphor or metonymy?) and theme (nature or artifice?) is what enables an arrival at this version of the real. Whether one calls the writing here extravagant or reckless, or both, it is precisely by the imprecision, and by the simultaneous employment and negation of the category of the beautiful, that O'Hara produces an extra, and seemingly novel category: the real.

From this brief passage, one discovers less about Pollock's painting than about the verbal imperatives of O'Hara's project. The account explicitly incorporates, as Pollock's painting does not, contingent, contemporary aspects of 1940s and 1950s New York life shared by both the poet and the painter: eroticism ("gigolo"), industry ("aluminum"), commercialism ("money"), cinema ("technicolor"), America/city ("big"), and the mass public ("vulgarity"). O'Hara tilts the named details toward excess and depravity such that positive artistic effects are linked, not to modernity *tout court,* but to a version of modernity that chafes against values of beauty. O'Hara chooses a traditionally aesthetic venue (here, nominally, painting) to explore a popular aesthetic of the real.

The poet's attraction to cinema as a popular mixed art form, and his frequent references and homages to the movies and film stars in his poetry, is crucial to understanding O'Hara's spin on the paradox of technology and poetry, so different from the aesthetically masked treatments of the question in Stevens and Bishop. Cinema, among "visual media"—an umbrella term which I stretch to include hybrid media like cinema and television—evolves the most sophisticated structural complex of post-industrial technology and modern art aesthetics. The movie experience is multi-faceted and cannot be reduced to its image component; it involves frequently shifting audience codes, viewing positions, habits of perceptual attention, duration and frequency of attendance, and commercially driven technological innovations. Further, with cinema we see the primacy of the fixed vertical image losing ground to the illusion of the continuously moving image. In the post-silent era, cinema expands to include diegetic voice, non-diegetic music, and all manner of sound effects.

Given how contingent these multiple aspects of cinema are upon technological production, it is thus with peculiar irony that O'Hara seizes on a "natural" visual scene, a sunset, in his account of Pollock's painting as cinematic. In writing that "the color is that of the sunset in a technicolor Western," he links "color" as an absolute abstract category to the commercial color production company, Technicolor. This move is significant not only insofar as O'Hara brings cinema into an equation with painting, but for the way O'Hara expressly isolates an element of film associated with artificiality, stylization, and commercialism. Film historian David Bordwell observes that Technicolor promoted its three-strip color process as a way to enhance the realism of *any* film; despite this advertising scheme, Hollywood was not convinced, and Technicolor quickly became identified with "the musical comedy, the historical epic, the adventure story, and the fantasy—in short, the genres of stylization and spectacle."[2] O'Hara mimes Hollywood logic by identifying technicolor with a sunset—the very naturalness and bright colors of which call attention to the artificiality of its reproduction—and further, with the Western, a genre that places a high value on idealized natural views of the American frontier.

Cinema inflects in multiple ways O'Hara's techni-poetic of the real. O'Hara saturates his poems with the "low," concrete, historically situated details of the Hollywood industry, film stars, and novelty technologies. This is an unexpected move in poetry: to privilege the referent with such excess and with a zest for the popular over the aesthetic, isolate, frozen image. Though O'Hara's work temporally overlaps with that of Stevens and Bishop in the postwar decade, he is part of a younger generation that conjures reality effects through a radically altered conception of the image. For the New York poets and action painters of O'Hara's milieu, a still-framed image is no longer the touchstone. "The axis of the image has changed," Krauss comments with regard to Pollock's shifting of the vertical axis of painting to horizontal, low, floor painting.[3] In the film industry during the postwar years, along with technicolor, one of the technological innovations adopted was similarly anti-vertical: cinemascope, which stretched the horizontal dimensions of the image, making expansive effects of landscape and epic breadth.

O'Hara's professed love of cinema in his mock manifesto of 1959, "Personism"[4]—"after all, only Whitman and Crane and Williams, of the American poets, are better than the movies"—is specifically made in balance with poetry. The American widescreen poets in the Whitman line, of which O'Hara gladly would count himself, promote the poet-individual as a participant in social, geographical, and contemporary experience at large. The celebrated personism upon which O'Hara's poetic effects depend is an outgrowth, I contend, of a high art embrace of the technological anti-aesthetic as a new kind of beauty—one that relies not upon a fixed subject and a static work of art, but a fluctuating moving presence. Effects of hyperrealism that I trace in O'Hara's poetry depend upon the foregrounding of artificial components, the reconfiguration of the poetic page as a kind of projecting screen, and linguistic simulation of 3-D emergence.

Positioned last in this three-author study, O'Hara is the figure who forces a collapse of the technology-poetry paradox forming the spine of this book; his work liberates readers and writers alike to broach the hermetic boundaries of poetry and to explore the fluid and interactive relations between media. O'Hara's poems are particularly situated—as in a seat in a movie theater—and to that extent, quite literal in their structure of spectatorship. His startlingly egoistic claim on the referent is the launching point not, as for Stevens, of objective language reality, nor as for Bishop, of the optically precise image, but of his own emergent personism. The marvel of his poetry, and one that accounts for O'Hara's current vogue, is that through the ruins, and the subversive undermining of high aesthetics, is the effect of Frank O'Hara himself, real poet.

> And here I am, the
> Center of all beauty!
> Writing these poems!
> Imagine! (*CP*, 11)

In this last stanza of "Autobiographia Literaria," O'Hara emphasizes the indexicality of "I," underscoring with triply exclamatory emphasis that it is true: "here I am." And the poem's last line, "Imagine!" is inflected with an irony that works against the romantic sense of seeing in the mind's eye: the flat, idiomatic recognition that something is true, "Imagine that." This effect of saying "I" has precedent in the nineteenth-century Anglo-American tradition in John Clare, Edgar Allan Poe, Christina Rossetti and others, but the peculiar potency of the O'Hara persona is the way it seems to emerge out of the page, as if into the room with us, through a precarious, ironic balance between hyper-materialist claims on the contingent, gritty details of commercial New York life, on the one hand, and overly emphatic claims upon beauty and selfhood, on the other.

This chapter develops further O'Hara's conflation of visual-verbal problems of representation, in this first section, as semiotically binding together his verbal art form with the visual art form of that of his abstract painter friends. This staged collapse in representational media is then transferred to the primary focus of this chapter, cinema and poetry, and to the structure of spectatorship O'Hara importantly locates in the movie theater. By his thematic choice to pair acts of reading with film viewing, I argue, O'Hara opens the way for poetry to explore representational effects of the real that break with poetry's inherited still-image model. In the section entitled "3-D," I consider how O'Hara integrates this peculiar Hollywood innovation, and the gimmicks of commercial overproduction more broadly, to graft lowbrow cinematic technology to his art form. The resulting techni-poetic effects include verbal effects in which numerous personae seem to pop out from the page, including O'Hara himself. Finally, I focus on the particular cathexis of the film star in O'Hara's work, and consider the unique opportunity for the marginal American poet, foreclosed from the dominant star system, at once to generate quasi-cinematic effects in poetry and to comment upon the hollowness within the flick.

"Why I Am Not a Painter," a disarmingly immediate, also funny, take on an issue that has plagued poets for centuries, sets the semiotic ground-work for the emergent O'Hara persona. Collapsing the differences between poetry or painting per se, O'Hara explores the bare bones of representation. The poem begins:

> I am not a painter, I am a poet.
> Why? I think I would rather be
> a painter, but I am not. (CP, 261)

The question posed by the title of the poem "Why I Am Not a Painter" is never expressly answered by the poem; the provided reason, because "I am not," merely repeats the terms of the question, twice. The negative "not," as traced in Stevens, and in O'Hara's account of Pollock ("it is not beautiful, but it *is* real"), is invoked to produce what *is*—in this case, the positive effect, "I am." The "I" appears nineteen times in this slender poem, and the sheer plurality produces a singular language effect, such that the unnamed

Frank seems to be frequently, through repetition, dropping into the poem. And this emergence is underscored, repeatedly, by the narrative account of the "I" literally going away and coming back in a series of visits to the studio of the named painter, "Mike Goldberg."

Well,

for instance, Mike Goldberg
is starting a painting. I drop in.
"Sit down and have a drink" he
says. I drink; we drink. I look
up. "You have SARDINES in it."
"Yes, it needed something there."
"Oh." I go and the days go by
and I drop in again. The painting
is going on, and I go, and the days
go by. I drop in. The painting is
finished. "Where's SARDINES?"
All that's left is just letters,
"It was too much," Mike says. (*CP*, 261–2)

In the first encounter, Frank observes after the fact that Mike has put "SARDINES" into his painting, and in the last, again after the fact, that he has dropped it. Elided from this narrative are the actual scenes where Mike puts "SARDINES" into his painting, and where he drops it. The second of the three instances of "I drop in" is where no encounter is recounted, and where the visit is embedded in five repetitions of "go" and "going"—akin to the auctioneer's idiomatic "going, going, gone." And indeed, in the narrative time between, the content disappears; Frank no longer sees "SARDINES," only their letters. But for the reader of the poem, the visual representation of the sardines never appeared to begin with; seeing "SARDINES" is the same as reading it. By keeping the word iconographically unchanged, O'Hara emphasizes how the effect of reading is the same whether the visual content is supposed to be there or not.

This ambiguity is rendered comic, as it often also is in Bishop, by the fact that actual drinking in the narrative ("I drink; we drink") precedes the "look" at something readable/visible that, beyond its effect, is actually edible. Prompting this structure of slippage between painting and poetry, or seeing and reading, is what O'Hara calls, with respect to Pollock, a "crisis of figuration" (*AC*, 35). And this crisis, as we will trace later in "To the Film Industry in Crisis," is brought on by a spread of commercialism, whereby the artist at once mimes and critiques the capitalist conversion of objects into products. O'Hara's conflation of monetary and aesthetic values overlaps with that of painterly and poetic values. The advertising that promises readiness for tangible consumption—"SARDINES"—is also what turns into the post-consumption material waste: the tin container without its contents. This absurdity is reproduced as an effect of painting, doubled by and within the effects of the poem.

A feeling of "too much," which may be prompted by an excess of commercial production (echoed later in the last stanza as its opposite, "There should be / so much more"), is answered by Mike's investment in too little, or nothing at all. By chiasmus, the product "SARDINES" is converted into a semiotic effect, and the effect into a product. The structure is one of emergence, where the spectator sits down and looks up, only to see/read "SARDINES" in the absence of any other context. Participating in this structure of emergence are not merely the products of art (still life, or, live fish or fruit), but the artists themselves—Frank and Mike as effects, the producers of art doubling as the products of art.

The reality effect of the "I" (Frank) is heightened through snatches of dialogue with "You" (Mike). The conversational tone of the whole of the poem seamlessly incorporates "actual" dialogue such that each word, in what reads less like a poem than live speech, acquires the status of a word-effect. Any modification of the "I" (such as details of dress, appearance, et cetera) would be too much, and would throw off the precarious balance of the effect of reading real words. Indeed, one effect of reading Frank O'Hara's poems is the sensation that he is, really and already, dropping in for a drink; we do not need him actually to appear, and in fact, his physical presence might be too much. The poem's third and last stanza—the Frank-half that structurally mirrors the Mike-half, in which opposites are also equivalents—acknowledges that the "I" has been the central focus all along. And as in the account of Pollock ("it is not beautiful, but it *is* real"), the grammatical structure of "is not . . . but . . . *is*," the fact that O'Hara is not a painter, but *is* a poet, turns out not to be a substitution of one state for another, but an equation of the two: not painter *and* poet, not beautiful *and* real.

> But me? One day I am thinking of
> a color: orange. I write a line
> about orange. Pretty soon it is a
> whole page of words, not lines.
> Then another page. There should be
> so much more, not of orange, of
> words, of how terrible orange is
> and life. Days go by. It is even in
> prose, I am a real poet. My poem
> is finished and I haven't mentioned
> orange yet. It's twelve poems, I call
> it ORANGES. And one day in a gallery
> I see Mike's painting, called SARDINES. (CP, 262)

O'Hara shifts from thoughts about the abstract color, "orange," by turning the color into a kind of commercial word-product of the page: "ORANGES." Part of O'Hara's wit here is that "orange" is known as a challenging word to rhyme in poetry. Here it is, in the plural—"ORANGES"—inside a poem, in a parallel position to "SARDINES." "Color" suddenly becomes like that of the sunset in a technicolor Western: bright, round, orange. And in shifting from the singular to the plural, O'Hara converts a single line of thought (color as an abstract category) into a material word-fruit for commercial consumption ("ORANGES" for publication, or to be hung in a gallery).[5] The reality effect of "ORANGES" is linked to O'Hara's effort to make the word not *like* oranges, but to make the word *be* oranges. This concentrated effort at denotation produces an excess of stylization—like that of technicolor, as opposed to mere color—in which the signified, returning as its own experience, is simultaneous with the effect of real oranges. This structure of pure denotation of the concrete detail, as examined via Barthes in the previous chapter, is carried over into the phrase: "I am a real poet." Conversational, idiomatic, as if drawn from real speech, the phrase materializes the "poet" into the "I" that "is," and as such, is "real." And the poem reveals itself as composed, not of lines, but of word-things that seem to pop three-dimensionally out of the page.

Neither oranges nor the poet, but the question of the relation between name (or title) and content, and the effect of the real produced in the slippages between them, is what is at stake here. Perloff observes that "Frank's art turns out to be just like Mike's,"[6] and this is true in a still deeper sense: "ORANGES" are not only like "SARDINES," a "poet" like a "painter," and "Frank" like "Mike," but each are effects of the poem—interchangeable as words to the extent that they share a semiotic structure in common. Each is a desirable by-product of the poem.

O'Hara's fascination with titles in "Why I Am Not a Painter" is significant given how sixty-odd poems in his oeuvre are without titles, save for the heading, "Poem." He makes the explicit comment in the Pollock monograph: "There is no need for titles." Even though he identifies with Pollock's style of titling, he could not merely emend his own twelve-part poem, "Oranges," to "*Number 12, 1953*," without losing the gimmick so vital to his project: non-correspondence between the appearance of the "real" word and the absence of "real" content. Precisely where O'Hara would seem to participate in an action painting ethos—writing poems that do not require titles because, as he explains for Pollock's paintings, each is "its own subject and the occasion for its expression"—is where we discover his interest in semiotic slippage and the play between things and names. The whole range of concrete details that make it into O'Hara's prolific body of poems, from oranges, technicolor, gigolos, vulgarity, to the "poet," contributes to his effects of emergence and figurative excess.

The all-important relation in cinema is that linking one image to the next, according to Christian Metz in "Photography and Fetish," whereas the privileged connection in still-photography is that of tying the image to the object it depicts.[7] O'Hara seems to generate emergence effects out of the crossing of these two lines of relation, insofar as they can be transferred onto word-to-object concerns (the still image tradition traced in Stevens and Bishop) and word-to-word concerns (Stein's language experiments). And this crossing of a still model of spectatorship with a moving model corresponds, historically, to the growth of technologically produced movement by machines, vehicles, and also the moving arts of cinema and video, and later, computer imagery.

Perloff insightfully, if cursorily, notes the significance of movement in O'Hara's aesthetic—why he loves the *motion* picture, *action* painting—and moreover his antipathy to static impressions.[8] In "To Hell With It," he writes "How I hate subject matter!" and continues ". . . all things that don't change, / photographs, / monuments . . ." (*CP*, 275). O'Hara's announced antipathy to photographs here, as well as his embrace of Abstract Expressionism and the cinema, does suggest that movement is a significant, but not exclusive, aspect of his production of reality effects. From a critical standpoint, O'Hara is best understood as a poet who generates effects of experiential poetry precisely through his resistance to mimetic structures. The effects explored in "Why I Am Not a Painter," as of objects (oranges, sardines) and of personae (Mike, Frank), derive from a composite structure of the still image and the moving image. The momentum of "I go" and "I go" is significantly punctuated by the still materialization of "I drop in."

Discussion of the cinema in O'Hara's poetry has been taken up by several critics, including Perloff, Vendler, Goldstein, and James Breslin. The principal limit of the analogy thus far results from a tendency to invoke a mimetic framework when making comparisons between poetry and the other arts. The assumption that Frank O'Hara writes poetry that is *like* other art forms—painting, photography, cinema, music—opens the possibility for a slippery substitution of one medium for another along shared grounds of likeness. Perloff writes of "Music" (1954), which opens *Lunch Poems*, that O'Hara employs a strategy of automatism of perception by "adapting the techniques of film and action painting to a verbal medium." A reference to modern dance is thrown in on top of film and action painting, and in the same discussion of O'Hara's mature period, Perloff describes his "Cubist syntax" and the affinity of his poetry with the music of John Cage. Each of these analogies is worthy of a study in its own right, but is here diffused by its own overdeterminacy in combination with the critic's underdeterminacy. Further, the imitative model Perloff adopts is incongruous with the critique of mimesis built into O'Hara's production of reality effects. When O'Hara conflates different art forms, as we saw in "Why I Am Not a Painter," he does so not for the sake of likeness, but rather to create an effect of emergence, of what "is," out of the tension between media.

Although far from a prophet of the avant-garde, Vendler is nonetheless savvy in her assessment of the project O'Hara is engaged in. While she complains that his poems lack a reason to stop, she admits that O'Hara is "a poet to be reckoned with, a new species."[9] Vendler's criticism shares in common with Perloff's a slippery, impressionistic set of comparisons to visual media; she can describe in the same paragraph O'Hara's poems as "photographic in their immediacy" and as "verbal movies." The distinction between the photographic and the cinematic is here elided, even as the role of movement in O'Hara's version of experiential immediacy crucially distinguishes it from a photographically oriented aesthetic.

Breslin goes further in probing O'Hara's stake in the cinema, commenting on the fanciful interest in cinematic stars of "The Three-Penny Opera." According to Breslin, O'Hara is not interested in a fixed reference point that distinguishes reality from the imaginary because he conceives of "reality itself [as] enigmatic, fictive, and theatrical."[10] Although I would modify this point to say that O'Hara *is* interested in fixed reference points (not to distinguish reality from the imaginary, but to accentuate ambiguity), I would also confirm the importance of Breslin's critical stance that O'Hara's version of reality incorporates the fictive into itself. Reality is already *mediated*, which is another way of saying that reality is an effect. The poet, at the interface with technical visual media, is more self-consciously inside the closed circle of effects than the film spectator. Ashbery writes in his prose poem, "The Lonedale Operator," that "somehow I was experienced the first time I saw a movie." The implications of Ashbery's comment are twofold: first, the postwar generation of poets grew up in a culture in which the pervasive influence of cinema touched the consciousnesses of those who had not yet even entered the movie theater; second, there is something inherent in the film medium, its "terror, or tedium," that renders virgin experience incongruous.[11] The next section considers how O'Hara thematizes his non-virgin status as a poet inside the movie theater.

SPECTATOR

Since its outset, film theory and criticism has been concerned to puzzle out what cinema brings that is new in our experience. Film theorists ranging from Bazin to Metz consider the role of indifference in the production of reality effects; feminist film theorists since the mid-seventies analyze spectatorial detachment; historians of cinema in recent years document technological innovation and changes in the motion picture industry that willy-nilly alter the spectator's experience. In some respects, O'Hara places himself in an analogous position to that of the film theorist. Breaking with a hermetic strain of the poetic tradition, and the criticism that leaves it lagging behind cultural change, O'Hara actively seeks to figure out what cinema brings that is new to the structure of artistic production. The link between poetry and cinema that I pursue is less a tool to interpret O'Hara's poetry than it is an opening into how O'Hara's poetry interprets.

Several of O'Hara's poems address the role and position of the spectator in the movie theater, "An Image of Leda," "Ave Maria," and "In the Movies" among them. Although each poem is radical in its own way, O'Hara introduces in each a shared structure of spectatorship. By overlapping the position of the cinema spectator with that of the poet/reader, O'Hara explores how the structure between the individual and the book—which prior to the computer age would seem to have an historically unshakeable aesthetic integrity—is altered by the new spectatorial role in the movie theater. Subversive eroticism, the revision of Catholicism or classical mythology, tension between media, tropes of black/white and seeing/blindness, and sight-touch divisions, are all part of O'Hara's cinematic phenomenology of the poem.

The structure of spectatorship offered in "An Image of Leda," the earliest and bleakest of O'Hara's poems on the cinema, aligns viewer and reader before "an empty white / space," and later, "under / this white eye." With the clarity of ambiguity traced in "Why I Am Not a Painter," O'Hara conflates differences between spectator and reader, even as he would seem to separate them out.

> The cinema is cruel
> like a miracle. We
> sit in the darkened
> room asking nothing
> of the empty white
> space but that it
> remain pure. And
> suddenly despite us
> it blackens. Not by
> the hand that holds
> the pen. There is
> no message. (*CP*, 35–36)

The phrase "despite us" is significant for the way it draws multiple referents under the same heading of spectator. In its broadest sense, "us" refers to the mass audiences attracted to American movie theaters in the late 1940s and early 1950s, including O'Hara himself, an avid movie-goer. In a more restricted sense, "us" refers to the readers of the poem who encounter a film screen that operates by principles foreign to those of the white page. And in a further sense, "us" implies an identity with the sexually passive, feminine position of Leda, as filtered through Yeats' sonnet of the Greek myth. The terms "we" and "us," all-embracing and empowering in other contexts, are used here as words "we" cannot get out from under. The poem sets in motion by short, declarative, enjambed lines, as if out of our control. The message it definitively offers, "There is / no message," contradicts the force of its own statement. How is the poem to be interpreted? O'Hara forces the question of the reader's singularity, making this public spectacle seem just awful enough in the context of the poem to make the reader want to get out from under this plurality, this "we." It is incumbent upon the reader to seek control, and to find sites of difference within affinity in order to discover where this sharply outlined structure of spectatorship is incomplete as a model of reading.

Here the black/white, light/dark trope, familiar from Stevens' Rome postcard and Bishop's "Seascape," is employed at a crucial moment. Film in "An Image of Leda" is a negative sublime, a "sin-ema." Like a miracle, it enacts an inhuman change or metamorphosis with or without the audience's participation, labor, or reflection. Unlike painting or poetry, it puts us face-to-machine with an anonymous "it," forcing the Foucauldian question for cinema: what is the author? The alarming observation that "suddenly despite us / it blackens," underscored by the fact that it is "Not by / the hand that holds / the pen," conveys the mixed feelings of bewilderment, defeat, and awe. A reversal of the situation in which the author generates light against darkness, here O'Hara stages the darkening and shadowing of the pure white page/screen.

"Despite," (from the Middle English "contempt, scorn" and the Latin "looking down on") points to a negative empowerment of the cinema machine and a corresponding diminishment of the human viewer who looks up to it. But what "we" as readers see, in the unexpected reversal O'Hara's poem forces upon us, are not images—the simulation of an actual movie on the screen—but ourselves *as* images.

> We our-
> selves appear naked
> on the river bank
> spread-eagled while
> the machine wings
> nearer. We scream
> chatter prance and
> wash our hair! (*CP*, 36)

O'Hara has us occupy the position of Leda, our hair in the river, overwhelmed by the machine-god, where technology substitutes for myth by force (in the logic predetermined by the myth). The projection of images that is part of the structure of reading is turned back upon itself by the literal projections of the moving picture: we are "read" as well as "spread-eagled" by the cinema machine. Spectator and reader alike are turned into

"An Image of Leda" by reverse projection, such that technology reverses myth, and film projects reading.

O'Hara reframes Yeats' question that closes his celebrated Leda sonnet as to whether she puts on the swan's power with his knowledge "Before the indifferent beak could let her drop?"[12] Where Yeats poses questions of power, knowledge, and history through sensuous images of a literal rape scene, of "thighs caressed" and "dark webs," O'Hara focuses them into the gap between touch and sight, dark and light, and the real and unreal—i.e., in a crisis of figuration prompted by cinema.

> Is
> it our prayer or
> wish that this
> occur? Oh what is
> this light that
> holds us fast? Our
> limbs quicken even
> to disgrace under
> this white eye as
> if there were real
> pleasure in loving
> a shadow and caress-
> ing a disguise! (*CP*, 36)

Unlike the flesh-to-flesh encounter of Yeats' sonnet ("He holds her helpless breast upon his breast"), this is an encounter in which one of the parties cannot be identified: "what is / this light / that holds us fast?" The attempt to identify, and to manifest physically, what remains elusively abstract— "this light"—produces this flesh-to-(what?) encounter. The gap between touch and sight, between caressing a body and caressing a "shadow" or "disguise," prompts O'Hara to bring in the key word, "real," at this juncture. He asks whether there is "real pleasure," and whether the pleasure itself is real, in caressing something that cannot be touched. What version of the real is it that we experience in this real-unreal hybrid? What kind of knowledge do we put on with cinema's power? The stance is ontological, for the question is not what cinema (and now, reading) is *like*, but what it *is*.

We are physically held fast—in our chairs—which makes this an apt point of comparison between reading and film. For poetry more often than not asks us to do this, to pretend to touch or to see something, like an "iris," when nothing is actually there. Cinema changes the rules of spectatorship in language. Before the empty white space of the cinema screen, O'Hara has us ask nothing except what is already lost (a virgin relation to reality); before the white space of the book, he has us ask something from it, something "real." This demand is not answered in this early poem the way it will be in O'Hara's mature work, of the period 1954 to 1966.

What is still to emerge is the flamboyant, vernacular, witty, name-dropping embrace of Hollywood, its film stars, and the movie theater of "To the Film Industry in Crisis": O'Hara's distinctive "personism." O'Hara is only half tongue-in-cheek when he declares a new movement in poetry: "I was realizing that if I wanted to I could use the telephone instead of writing the poem, and so Personism was born . . .. The poem is at last between two persons instead of two pages" (*CP*, 499). The telephone plays a similar function to that of the cinema as a technology that invites O'Hara's irreverently humorous, and scandalizing acceptance, of radical changes in communication.

Operative points of departure in the development of O'Hara's later style are the dehumanizing character of the cinema and the technological pro-duction of reality. Ashbery comments on the element of O'Hara's work that "simply doesn't care."[13] Indifference, in the context of postwar aes-thetic experience, is a crucial term; one of O'Hara's considerable talents is to manipulate indifference, an attitude inculcated into the film spectator, into a positive hybrid experience of noncontradictory opposites: passivity and activity, private and public, unreal and real, intangible and tangible, reading and seeing.

Part of the spectatorial charm of cinema is the ease with which audiences can overlook the erotically charged nature of the experience. Particularly during the 1950s, when O'Hara was frequenting the cinema sometimes daily, movie theaters in Manhattan held many of the attractions of the old-style movie palaces: grand screening halls with plush seats, ushers, and an impressive display of technical novelties. Such an atmosphere maximizes sensory gratification and physical comfort, while at the same time promis-ing a high degree of anonymity. Rather than comfortably overlooking these aspects of the cinema, O'Hara takes an opposite stance: he makes hyper-bolic advances toward the movie theater as an outlet for socio-sexual desires. In converting the paradoxically publicly closeted eroticism of cine-matic experience into a viable subject for poetry, O'Hara at the same time grants poetry the privileged place of critique and validation of what is new with this popular visual medium.

Viewed from the strikingly different perspective O'Hara increasingly adopts over the course of his two-decade career, anonymity and indiffer-ence are the ripe occasions for non-culturally-endorsed sexual play. Hollywood's promotion of normative, heterosexual values in no way hin-ders O'Hara from exploring the eroticism *between* the viewer and the screen. This is a radical move, to the point of being threatening for some readers. By naming the movie theater and its film stars rather than the more pedestrian settings (bars, newspaper stands, train stations) that tend to dominate his verse, O'Hara effectively places his poetry in the center of debates in popular culture. A distinction of O'Hara's poetry of the cinema, then, is the way he foregrounds aspects of sexuality that mass American culture is inclined to view negatively

O'Hara would loosen up the attitude not only toward what is erotically permissible in the cinema, but toward what is worthy of his personal, poetic notarization. "Ave Maria," the much-loved O'Hara poem that makes the plea, "Mothers of America / let your kids go to the movies!," (*CP*, 371) identifies the "darker joys" of the movie theater as masturbation and pre-adolescent sex with strangers. The movie theater substitutes for the Catholic confessional, as O'Hara confounds the priest's role of absolving sins with the oft-ignored, less savory sexual exploitation of young boys. The structure is akin to the mimetic desire within O'Hara's James Dean elegies, in which the narrator's own homoerotic investment is deflected and triangulated through a female muse. Here the choice of the American mother as the unlikely Christian Mary is perhaps O'Hara's oblique strategy to release himself from the maternal and religious constraints of his own upbringing. He brilliantly schemes in "Ave Maria" to render the mother blameworthy if she does not validate a gay pick-up scene.

A witty and daring experiment with the ode form, the poem directly addresses the American mother as the protector of mainstream values. It would be "unforgivable" to keep the kids from going to the movies, the poem concludes, "so don't blame me if you won't take this advice / and the family breaks up / and your children grow old and blind in front of a TV set / seeing / movies you wouldn't let them see when they were young" (*CP*, 372). O'Hara emphasizes the paradox that one grows blind while seeing, and turns it to the advantage of cinema. He humorously holds out the television set as the ultimate signifier of family break-up, while the movie theater is what holds the peaceful family together. But the deeper blindness, the blinding of the imagination that comes from too much seeing (and consequently, never enough), is embedded into the poem only through a doubled layer of irony. Since the comparison is between cinema and television, the question of poetry emerges only through the hyberbolic embrace of the movie theater; and what emerges over and above this excessive language is the effect of the "poem."

O'Hara adds to this the transgressive proposition that it is not the movie itself, but the occasion the movie theater provides for the kid's "first sexual experience" ("which only cost you a quarter"), that serves as the necessary glue for normative American life. O'Hara subverts the logic of Catholicism, and converts the lexicon of "forgiveness" and "blame" into a sexual release from societal restraints. O'Hara would turn the dichotomies of heaven and hell into a new religious sublime, in which the values of black and white, whether in the theater or poem, are erotically charged with the promise of a dark theater.

In "In the Movies," O'Hara explores the erotic stimuli of ushers, masseur seats, and flesh on the screen. He contemplates the various sites of slippage in the flesh-to-image encounter at the center of O'Hara's structure of spectatorship. Mere seeing does not sufficiently satisfy cinema's invitation to tactility and erotic satisfaction. Optical sight is exposed as an ambiguous and faulty measure of the mixed experiences of desire and revulsion, inspiration and boredom, that constitute catching an afternoon flick in Times Square. Entering the ravine between seeing and caressing, O'Hara, like his fellow poets, finds the mismatch between sight and touch pivotal to a verbal account of twentieth-century sensory experience. O'Hara's synaesthetic focus in "In the Movies" doubles as a lack of focus, in which sight exchanges with touch, flowers with faces, and screen with page. The space between the viewer and the screen is charged as a nebulous zone, worthy of a long poem, for exploring effects of merging and emerging.

> Out of the corner of my eyes
> a tear of revulsion sighs,
> it's the point of intersection a foot in front of me,
> I call it my cornea, my Muse.
> I hurl myself there—at whatever fatal flowery flourish!
> flower? flower?
> if that face is flourishing, it's toes of tin!
> Well, but there is a face there, a ravine of powder and gasps,
> I can see it, I must caress it. (*CP*, 206–207)

The "point of intersection" clarifies nothing; it could be literally his own foot in front of him in the dark movie theater, or the "plumes of your penis," as so named later in the poem. The ambiguity as to what to call "it" ("my cornea, my Muse") depends on how it is seen. Is it a cornea, and therefore a purely optical extract of the body, displaced from the body and seen as an image of itself, like Bishop's "iris-beds"? Or is it a Muse, an abstraction that visibly materializes as the poem, on the page a foot in front of us? The various subjects—"tear," "cornea," "Muse," "flower," and "face"—do not intersect, but are suspended as if in three dimensions, in the nebulous intermediary zone between the viewer and screen. And this complicates the question of what we are supposed to be literally seeing, whether *in* the movies, or *in* the poem.

Cinematic movement is crucially optical, and lacking in any actual, tangible content. But Metz points out that this visuality is a characteristic of movement in general, brought only to a new extreme by cinema. Tangibility is not part of the appearance of the movement, either on or off screen. This point enables Metz to claim that cinematic movement is "a second production belonging to the same order of reality."

The strict distinction between object and copy dissolves on the threshold of motion. Because movement is never material but is *always* visual, to reproduce its appearance is to duplicate its reality. In truth, one cannot even 'reproduce' a movement; one can only re-produce it in a second production belonging to the same order of reality, for the spectator, as the first.[14]

That is, what the spectator perceives is not merely a reproduction of actual movement, but movement itself, "there it is." Paradoxically, this model grants more seemingly tangible reality to the sense of vision, even as it forecloses actual touch. Further, unlike the postcard and the stereoscope, which also generate this disconnection between sight and touch, the cinema does it by the means in which it normally happens *in reality*.

O'Hara casts the fatal flourish of the cinema screen in "In the Movies" as its invitation to fleshly desires in the absence of a corporeal body. This structure, as the poem communicates at several moments, is shared by the poetic page. The literal space of the poem—the book—has nothing of the accoutrements of the movie theater, with its ushers, plush seats, and other spectators. But O'Hara takes up two of the most popular motifs in poetry, flowers and birds, and through the repetition of "flowers" and "plumes," plays with materializing them—as if to have them emerge from out of the page. But since the location of "flowers" and "plumes" is never exact, because O'Hara introduces so many lines of projection, and conflicting points of intersection, their emergence effects have all the certainty of one of Bishop's "stereoscopic views." The plumes literally go up in smoke at the poem's close, as the spectator's pleasure ("born from this projection") comes at the cost of the spectator turning ghostlike ("the smoke of my death"). And the repetition of "flower? flower?" that gathers the momentum of a refrain in the first few stanzas is replaced in the fourth by the seemingly more material bodies, "Ushers! Ushers!" Borrowing the style of expression from Whitman, and the peripheral look as if from Bishop, O'Hara, from his chair in the movie theater, looks for real bodies out of the corner ("cornea") of his eye (*CP*, 207–209).

O'Hara offers a hyperrealistic answer to the question posed in "An Image of Leda" as to whether the cinema offers "real pleasure." The concrete movie theater does, even if the screen images offer only hybrids of the real/unreal. In exploring the physical sensations produced in the spectator, and the phenomenological relation to this "ravine of powder and gasps," O'Hara considers the possibilities of not-being-there as a precondition for another actuality. The logic of the phrase, "I can see it, I must caress it," is a failed logic not only in the face of cinema, but in the face of poetry.

> There seems to be a ghost up there,
> Brushing off his gems and plumes.
> [. . .]
> And as the plumes flutter in the current they spell out * * * * *

but I don't believe my eyes, it's only a ghost's habit.
I bought a ticket so I could be alone. With the plumes.
With the ushers. (*CP*, 207)

The iconographic stars, in lieu of the costumes of the film stars, create a visual moment in which what is spelled out in print is *seen*. And this seeing prompts a disbelief, "I don't believe my eyes"—a recognition of ghostliness, both in viewing and in reading. Like Stevens' ghostly Reading postcard, and its poetic companion, "Large Red Man Reading," the cinema's half-present, half-absent fluttering plumes are also plumes for writing—in the available typeface—what cannot be uttered, but only read/seen.

The referential ambiguity O'Hara balances with such precision in a conversational mode, as examined in "Why I Am Not a Painter," here falls into a synaesthetic uncertainty of reference. The logic of describing one sense in terms of another, in which words circulate between the five senses to express something, is turned upon the relation between poem and movie. The complexity of the lines, "like a poem written in blackface, / his flower opens and I press my face into the dahlialike mirror," derives not only from a crossing between sight and touch—between facing something and being tactilely in its face—but between page and screen. Falling into the chiasm between "like . . . face" and "face . . like" is the poem as "blackface" and the film as "dahlialike." If cinema gives us visible flowers, and poetry relative obscurity, each reflect our own faces and projected desires. As a poet in the movie theater, O'Hara stages an erotic crossing within a shared structure of spectatorship: the cinema offers itself as the erotic other, as light projected against blackness, to one who writes in black on white.

3-D

In the early 1950s, the Hollywood film industry began to make widespread use of novelty technologies such as Cinemascope, Technicolor and 3-D. The reasons were manifold: an expansiveness of the marketplace after Depression-era and war-time economies; the rising competition posed by television entering American households; a newfound audience receptivity to enhanced illusions and encompassing sensory effects. The seemingly most obvious factor contributing to this shift—namely, that the technologies became available—is ironically the least applicable. Jean-Louis Comolli makes the convincing argument in "Machines of the Visible" that changes in cinematic techniques are more ideologically motivated than they are the result of fresh technological inventions.[15] Bordwell confirms this theory, pointing out in his film history of Hollywood that "widescreen cinema was technically feasible at least two decades before its acceptance."[16] Widescreen was first introduced in 1929, and 70mm film became available in 1933.

Something intrinsic to the climate of the early 1950s, then, spurred film producers to take the gamble they had previously been unwilling to take— that the expense of such technological enhancements would repay itself by attracting larger audiences to the movie theaters. The gamble worked, and the atmosphere of movie theaters at the time was unique. Spectators were exposed to a high degree of technical experimentation within a relatively concentrated period of time. Notably, these experiments with heightening sensory illusions in the movie theater took place against a back-drop of strict political control. The film industry's most concentrated effort to recapture audiences occurred during the McCarthy years of 1950 to 1954, when the structure of spectatorship as to what was real, and what was merely projected, was mirrored as a structure of anxiety in the American political climate. Ashbery, then a young poet and close friend to O'Hara also living in New York, writes chillingly about the experience of being a homosexual during this period, and of the fear that his fate was not his to control (Gooch, 190). O'Hara's description of the "white eye" of the cinema suggests how easily spectatorial pleasures could flip over into paranoia.

Although O'Hara gives the impression of being less affected by the climate of paranoia, he does question in "An Image of the Leda" the masochism of the film spectator. Indeed, there is a certain undeniable paradox that a famously promiscuous gay poet during the McCarthy era should be so attracted to a film culture dictated by Hollywood norms and strict social and sexual prohibitions. Hollywood is after all one of the culprits in dictating normative experience, and further, in coding that experience heterosexual. But O'Hara, in contrast with Ashbery, seemed to have little trouble reconciling his private gay world with normative American culture. When O'Hara was enlisted in the navy in 1944, for example, he was exposed to propaganda films, or what he referred to as "Why We Fight" movies. O'Hara's report of the experience does not concern the overwhelming messages of these films, but rather his enthusiasm for the accompanying Beethoven score. Not until he was stationed in Key West, Florida, and was seeing such movies as a large-scale Technicolor production of *Kismet* starring Marlene Deitrich, did O'Hara write home that he was returning to normal (Gooch, 60–67).

The climate of the fifties in Manhattan for the so-called New York School Poets[17] was rife with contradictions. Both Ashbery and O'Hara were attracted to the artistic culture of the day, particularly painting, but for O'Hara, the movie theater was an especially addictive cultural phenomenon. O'Hara was fascinated with the kind of Hollywood cinema that featured Cinemascope, Vistavision, Technicolor, Stereophonic Sound, and the other technologies under experimentation in the postwar period. In "To the Film Industry in Crisis," his poem of 1957 that addresses the crisis, not of McCarthyism, but of television, O'Hara writes that we must all decide to whom to give our love in times of crisis:

> [. . .] not to the Catholic Church
> Which is at best an oversolemn introduction to cosmic entertainment,
> Not to the American Legion, which hates everybody, but to you,
> glorious Silver Screen, tragic Technicolor, amorous Cinemascope,
> stretching Vistavision and startling Stereophonic Sound, with all
> your heavenly dimensions and reverberations and iconoclasms!

O'Hara' histrionic modifications—"glorious," "tragic," "amorous," "stretching," "startling"—are a willful abuse of the poetic value of the precisely chosen word. This is a techni-poetic drawn from film industry advertising; O'Hara cultivates an unnaturally personal relation to artificial production. From the excessive performativity of the film star (to be examined in this chapter's last section) and the emotive responses of film audiences, O'Hara generates a quasi-love between us as viewers/readers, and the impersonal, technical novelties of contemporary cinema. O'Hara produces this hybrid human-to-machine relationship, part emotional, part commercial, out of the materials provided by commercial cinema—principally, the advertised innovations of stylization and spectacle.

A brief history of one such innovation—3-D—bears witness to this bizarre period in American cinema that caught O'Hara's fancy. Of the cinematic techniques being tried out on film audiences, 3-D most approximates gimmickry. 'Natural Vision' 3-D was introduced in 1952. Its most distinctive feature is the effect of emergence, and advertising campaigns promised the shock value of an apparently three-dimensional hand or object emerging out of the movie screen towards the spectator. The colored glasses that are necessary to produce a strong effect of three-dimensionality—an effect cinema achieves on its own only minimally—are material artifacts of cinema's claim to make illusion real. 3-D glasses are a tangible reminder that vision is mediated, and that the space between viewer and screen is not a "pure" space between eyes and object. 3-D effects are channeled, not into the storyline, but into the creation of suspended moments, in which one is aware of the act of looking at the image. A challenge to Metz's point that "the strict distinction between object and copy dissolves on the threshold of motion," 3-D rematerializes the relation between object and copy as both a problem and pleasure of cinema. And this is O'Hara's challenge as well, to make coexist an experiential art that claims to be part of reality (cinematic movement or action painting) *and* a precariously mimetic art that focuses on the relation between object and copy.

To the extent that vivid effects of 3-D raise awareness of the very structure of spectatorship, they resemble the stereoscopic effects I discussed in the previous chapter. The illusion of three-dimensionality calls attention to representational failure because the spectator is reminded that he or she is being invited to *use* the simulacrum to fool him or herself. How does this work? The logic of the eye is such that vision persists after the image is gone; light stays on the retina longer than it does in reality (which explains why one sees light spots with closed eyes). In other words, the eye *forgets* that what it sees is only the after-image of what is no longer present. Optical illusions operate on this principal that we forget that what we are seeing is an illusion once in the midst of it. Comolli fine-tunes this point with the seemingly obvious, but easily forgotten, observation that we both forget and we do not; it is not only possible to do both at once, but unavoidable. "There is no spectator other than the one *aware* of the spectacle," he writes, "even if (provisionally) allowing him or herself to be taken in by the fictioning machine, deluded by the simulacrum: it is precisely *for that* that he or she came" (Comolli, 139). Forgetfulness in the movie theater, then, is at most a mixed and fluid condition, wherein the spectator retains on some level an awareness that he or she is participating in an illusion.

Cinemascope, Vistavision, Technicolor, Stereophonic Sound, 3-D, Sense-Surround, and the other technologies under experimentation during a concentrated period in the 1950s simultaneously accentuate the power of cinematic illusion *and* the spectator's participation in that illusion. This paradox is further underscored by Comolli's theoretical assertion that cinema, more than other representative mediums that precede it (theater, painting, photography, etc.):

> "precisely because it effects a greater approximation to the analogical reproduction of the visible . . . is no doubt more profoundly, more decisively undermined than those other apparatuses by everything that separates the real from the representable and even the visible from the represented." (Comolli, 141)

The shock effect of a hand reaching out of the movie screen produces a powerful illusion, but one almost entirely lacking in the capacity to retain the enduring interest of audiences. This is because the delicately balanced social and physiological mechanism whereby the spectator willingly dupes his or herself, and simultaneously retains an awareness that he or she is doing so, is upset by the over-pronounced reality effect of 3-D. Hyperreality, as was observed of Bishop's optical effects, has a polarizing effect on the way we process visual illusions. 3-D shares with the stereoscope the destiny of quickly becoming obsolete, only being revived every decade or so since the 1950s. It captured the attention of film audiences for little over a year, and within three years, was dead.

It is worth considering in this context precisely why Frank O'Hara was so attracted to the big production films of the 1950s. Two important terms that recur in his writings on the cinema are "vulgarity" and "immediacy." In a little poem called "My Heart," which just precedes "To the Film Industry in Crisis" in the *Collected Poems*, O'Hara plays on the division between popular and high art to express "Frank" as a composite effect of contradictions.

> I'm not going to cry all the time
> nor shall I laugh all the time,

> I don't prefer one "strain" to another.
> I'd have the immediacy of a bad
> movie, not just a sleeper, but also the big,
> overproduced first-run kind. I want to be
> at least as alive as the vulgar. And if
> some aficionado of my mess says "That's
> not like Frank!", all to the good! I
> don't wear brown and grey suits all the time,
> do I? No. I wear workshirts to the opera,
> often. I want my feet to be bare,
> I want my face to be shaven, and my heart—
> you can't plan on the heart, but
> the better part of it, my poetry is open. (*CP*, 231)

O'Hara employs the term "vulgar" in its contemporary sense of unrefined, coarse, and in bad taste, as well as in its Latinate sense from *vulgaris*, meaning 'common people.' O'Hara's poetry is nothing if not of the popular vernacular, and some have even wondered if as such, it even counts as poetry.[18] Here the tone is conversational, and the language is thoroughly and recognizably that of popular speech. It is immediate and it is vulgar in a way that would have shocked many of his poetic predecessors.[19] Yet even as O'Hara has by this point shaven off most of the residual Yeatsian high talk encountered in "An Image of Leda," his theme of the "heart" is one of the oldest in poetry. Just as O'Hara would both laugh and cry, be clean-shaven and barefoot, and wear workshirts to the opera, he would project himself as both a poet and an ordinary guy.

Precisely the contradiction that the big spectacle films offer, that they make a claim on both art and commercial screening, is the kind of leap of logic that O'Hara makes with respect to the "natural vulgarity" of the Pollock painting. Further, the kind of movie experience O'Hara identifies with his self-projected "I" is the "big, over-produced" kind—a characterization that might easily substitute for that of "*Number 12, 1952*" as "big, brassy." O'Hara seeks to conflate private and public, high and low art, in this double-striding "I" with his two-part heart.

The movie theater and the city both invite this interface of public and private. The spectator sits in a crowded movie theater with a lot of other people, and that theater is probably located in a city if it has a budget large enough to accommodate technological innovations. Cinematic immediacy, of the first-run, overproduced kind specified above, is linked to the city, and to what O'Hara elsewhere calls "life-giving vulgarity." City life is a link for the cinematic extremes evident in O'Hara's work: on the one hand, vulgarity and immediacy, and on the other, the indifference of a spectacle that rolls on with or without the participation of any one individual. O'Hara is a consummate poet of city life, and his refusal to live anywhere but Manhattan from 1951 onwards confirms that the city is fundamentally constitutive of his aesthetic. Part of the appeal, and even necessity, of being in the city for O'Hara seems to be the experience of its excess. Signs of overproduction everywhere call attention to the fact of the city as artifice.

Consider the following lines from O'Hara's "Having a Coke with You": "in the warm New York 4 o'clock light we are drifting back and forth / between each other like a tree breathing through its spectacles" (*CP*, 360). The arbitrary image of a tree with spectacles matches the arbitrariness of there *being* a tree in the city. City details require something like the special glasses used for 3-D; they share with the overproduced movies of the fifties a hyperrealism that draws attention to the underlying structure of artifice. An individual walking the city streets, at least someone who has lived outside of a city like O'Hara, carries no illusions about sincerity or naturalness. An awareness is maintained, on some level, that the visible reality of the city is constructed rather than given. The city scene is one of many possible visible realities, and the fact that the one currently before the eyes consumes the attention, does not entirely cover over that it is a constructed reality. O'Hara seems to thrive on precisely this sensation of artifice, writing in "Meditations in an Emergency":

> I have never clogged myself with the praises of pastoral life, nor with nostalgia for an innocent past of perverted acts in pastures. One need never leave the confines of New York to get all the greenery one wishes—I can't even enjoy a blade of grass unless I know there's a subway handy, or a record store or some other sign that people do not totally *regret* life. It is more important to affirm the least sincere; the clouds get enough attention as it is and even they continue to pass. (*CP*, 197)

Altieri asserts that the defining feature of O'Hara's work is "presence," and qualifies this presence as being of a city variety. Presence in the city is antithetical to presence in nature, according to Altieri, because "city details . . . have neither meaning, hierarchy, nor purpose not created absolutely by man."[20] Altieri takes the proliferation of proper names as a signal of a poetry without content, and O'Hara's city landscape as one lacking depth or inner reality. The point is convincing, though it overstates the case for systemlessness; artifice is not without a system, as O'Hara's work underscores. His poetic effects depend upon the manipulation of a system of illusions, borrowed from technology, from the city, from contemporary life, and they depend also upon a critique of a lack at the core of these illusions.

Further, O'Hara stages a structure of spectatorship wherein the reader/viewer's passivity and the cinema's mechanical indifference combine to produce reality effects of vitality, emotion, and personality. One might even say that the O'Hara persona is excessive, hyper, and prone to creating effects that distract from content. This, I propose, is a technique he absorbs from the Hollywood cinema of his day. To trace this logic, recall the terms of the poem, "An Image of Leda": the cinema is "cruel like a miracle"; it happens "despite us"; "there is no message." At an opposite extreme from most of O'Hara's poems on the cinema, "An Image of Leda" is anonymous insofar as it is entirely without reference to a particular film, theater, or movie star. It is a poem about the cinema *qua* medium, and its emphasis is on the extent to which we, despite the "despite us," are willing participants in its particular system of illusions.

O'Hara confirms the self-chosen aspect of his cinema-going with a quasi-certitude of reference, declaring his love at the opening of "To the Film Industry in Crisis," not to books, theater, and opera, but to the Motion Picture Industry.

> Not you, lean quarterlies and swarthy periodicals
> With your studious incursions toward the pomposity of ants,
> Nor you, experimental theatre in which Emotive Fruition
> Is wedding Poetic Insight perpetually, nor you,
> Promenading Grand Opera, obvious as an ear (though you
> Are close to my heart), but you, Motion Picture Industry,
> it's you I love! (*CP*, 232)

The grammatical structure is by now familiar as the "not . . . but" logic of O'Hara's account of Pollock's painting, in which the choice of what is "real" instead of "beautiful" ("it is not beautiful, but it *is* real") is actually a recognition of their simultaneity. "Poetic Insight" can coexist with the "Motion Picture Industry," even though insight would seem to be in contradiction with industry, and its too visible pictures and its too real motions.

STAR

Already in the declaration "it's you I love!" O'Hara manages to insert his self-exclamatory "I" into a commercial side of cinema that is antagonistic to personal individuals and manipulative of the emotion of love. But of course there is a more personally oriented side of the cinema that accounts for much of its success as a medium: the phenomenon of the film star. From the relative anonymity of the film spectator (despite O'Hara's efforts to reclaim the spectator's individuality and tangibility), O'Hara pivots to questions of the personally stamped, and irreplaceably individual, film star. The structure of spectatorship that we have examined thus far for its emergence effects is here most explicitly tilted toward emergence of the individual, whether the poet, the film star, or both, in the ambiguous verbal-visual space between.

O'Hara makes a brilliant gesture in "To the Film Industry in Crisis" to address the cinema in the form of an ode. The range of responses to the "crisis" the cinema poses to poetry, as O'Hara sees it, is fairly limited: on the one hand, you can lament the loss of a personal message and the cruelty of a medium that rolls on without you; on the other, you can rival it, celebrate it, and/or laugh at it, as he does here. His semi-ironic declaration of personal love flung against the impersonal, money-driven medium, has a high entertainment value. The cinema as divinity loses its malevolence, and the excess is all on the side of the appreciative spectator. The fifties fantasy of cinematic excess meets its match, and impersonality is converted into personality. This is accentuated by the transference of love from the industry to the film star. O'Hara makes a quantum leap from "An Image of Leda" by substituting the oppressive singularity of the "white eye" of the cinema screen with a materially profuse parade of personalities, each striking a distinctive personal pose.

                                                                                To
> Richard Barthelmess as the "tol'able" boy barefoot and in pants,
> Jeanette MacDonald of the flaming hair and lips and long, long neck,
> Sue Carroll as she sits for eternity on the damaged fender of a car
> and smiles, Ginger Rogers with her pageboy bob like a sausage
> on her shuffling shoulders, peach-melba-voiced Fred Astaire of the feet,
> Eric von Stroheim, the seducer of mountain-climbers' gasping spouses,
> the Tarzans, each and every one of you (I cannot bring myself to prefer
> Johnny Weissmuller to Lex Barker, I cannot!), Mae West in a furry sled,
> her bordello radiance and bland remarks, Rudolph Valentino of the moon,
> Miriam Hopkins dropping her champagne glass off Joel McCrea's yacht
> and crying into the dappled sea, Clark Gable rescuing Gene Tierney
> from Russia and Allan Jones rescuing Kitty Carlisle from Harpo Marx,
> Cornel Wilde coughing blood on the piano keys while Merle Oberon berates,
> Marilyn Monroe in her little spike heels reeling through Niagra Falls,
> Joseph Cotton puzzling and Orson Welles puzzled and Dolores del Rio
> eating orchids for lunch and breaking mirrors, Gloria Swanson reclining,
> and Jean Harlow reclining and wiggling, and Alice Faye reclining
> and wiggling and singing, Myrna Loy being calm and wise, William Powell
> in his stunning urbanity, Elizabeth Taylor blossoming, yes, to you

> and to all you others, the great, the near-great, the featured, the extras
> who pass quickly and return in dreams saying your one or two lines,
> my love! (*CP*, 232)

In lieu of the alienated viewer of a cruel cinema, O'Hara is now the synthesizer and charismatic director of dozens of film stars, each in the midst of striking his or her own characteristic gesture. How to register this change? The increasingly confident, egoist poet is here maximizing the personal and vulgar elements of the cinema and matching them with all the excesses and showiness he can muster from poetry. The depersonalizing effects of the cinema are incorporated into a blithe embrace of Hollywood's multiple personalities.

By opting for the ode form, a vehicle for public utterance, O'Hara adapts the material to the occasion; he complies with the expected tone of the ode as "emotional, exalted, and intense," and the subject matter as "whatever divine myths can be adduced to the occasion." The apocalyptic threat of cinema is replaced by the pleasures of revering celluloid gods, and the lapsed Catholic's lifelong exposure and openness to the experience of the movie theater converts into this semi-ironic, public profession of love for America's linked religions of cinema and money.

The mystery of why audiences are drawn back to the movie theater, even as it happens "despite us," achieves resolution in the figure of the film star. As a cult, the cinema is endowed with the greatest power to attract audiences when it offers a figure for reverence. O'Hara focuses on one such figure in his tributes to James Dean, so it is noteworthy that here he opts to touch down glancingly upon a multiplicity of stars. Jim Ellege sees the cinema in O'Hara's poetry as a vehicle for love, pointing out that the homosexual O'Hara "ironically chose a decidedly heterosexual medium by which to investigate love."[21] To the extent that one wants to name the emotional intensity of "To the Film Industry in Crisis" as "love," (Ellege attributes "perfect love" to the cinema), it seems worth investigating what kind of love could possibly prompt this speaker to address so many film stars seemingly in a single breath. The Whitmanesque sweep O'Hara achieves in the poem need only be mustered in the face of a comparably momentous subject. The force of ambivalence and ironic distance that the cinema imposes requires that the viewer hurl his affections outward at a medium that is indifferent to all except the demands of capitalism. This is perhaps one version of love, but it is not a reciprocal one. The naming of the film stars seems to have the effect of personalizing the distance, even rendering it amorous.

O'Hara's approach is more meditated and systematic than its spontaneous effusions would have us believe. The assembling of film stars, under the category of the "film industry," is meant to be enabling of the audiences of both film and poetry. Although the proper names scattered throughout O'Hara's oeuvre can have a slightly alienating effect, the sheer number increases the probability that we will recognize some. In this poem, O'Hara's invitation to his personal network is cast widely, for the set of references is one in which most every American has some stake. Certainly the tone and rhythm of the ode are meant to include the audience in a publicly shared enthusiasm.

O'Hara maximizes the degree of audience participation by inviting us into his capacious personal history of movie-going. The multiple references, some of which are pulled from his childhood movie experiences in the 1930s, invite memory testing of proper names. The reader is made an insider to the experience of the poem. O'Hara makes no attempt to have that experience be synonymous with, or even mimetic of, the experience of being in the movie theater. But he does attempt to rally our affections and to rekindle our desire to go to the movies through a series of star-images that function in much the same way as fan photos of movie stars.

From a more or less shared pool of mental images, each of the fragmentary shots—"Ginger Rogers with her pageboy bob," or "Jean Harlow reclining and wiggling"—function as a synecdoche for the entire film persona. Recent film theory observes that the star photo is always incomplete because it offers only the still image, whereas the cinema offers the synthesis of voice, body and motion. As such, the star photo is an invitation to the cinema: the "completion of its lacks, the synthesis of its separate fragments."[22] But seen from another angle, the verbal "snapshots" O'Hara generates of multiple film stars actually work like suspended moments within the continuous motion of film. Such moments, as discussed with respect to 3-D, draw our awareness to the film (or its stars) as construct.

By highlighting the object-copy divide that is in part obscured or forgotten by the powerful experientialism of cinema, O'Hara draws attention to faulty mimetic structure. But by creating the momentum and accumulation of a seemingly unstoppable and continuous list of stars, he simultaneously and in contradiction invokes second-order reality of cinematic movement for the poem.

I want to propose that the traits which O'Hara's poetry shares with cinema—excess, vulgarity, movement, presence—all emphasize the active participation of the reader. The poetry energizes the reader to respond to surroundings, however increasingly depersonalized they may be, with flair, and to synthesize rather than feel alienated by the fragmented nature of postwar experience. O'Hara's seemingly random, entropic profession of affections and observations should not delude his readers. He is engaged in a meditated project of producing effects of the real that makes the cinema a large participant in the kind of poetry he writes. Precisely O'Hara's receptivity to his times, and to the mass culture of the city, prompts him to respond fluidly and consciously to what could not but be an influence in the work of every poet writing in the postwar period. The specific fact about O'Hara is that it is Hollywood's most flamboyant and spectacular style of cinema that has the greatest influence on his development of an ars poetica.

The Hollywood stylization of film is associated as much with individual stars like Marilyn Monroe, James Dean, and Elizabeth Taylor as with particular technical features. O'Hara rises to the challenge with a persona-on-the-page that can compete with such star power. But the outspoken loudness of the persona he adopts is not necessarily contradictory, by O'Hara's own logic, with the muted, soft-spoken characteristics he named and identified within the figure of James Dean. By the same logic, the lifelike presence of the film stars O'Hara so loved is not incompatible with the real corporeal absences of the actual individuals toward whom O'Hara felt a love that might also be called necrophilia.

O'Hara's poems generated a small scandal in the mid-1950s when a series of elegies to James Dean were published. A similar gesture to that of

"The Day the Lady Died," in which the subject of Billie Holiday ensures that everyone reading has an opinion or associative memory, O'Hara's choice to match popular culture with the death of a celebrity ensures that readers will pay attention. Aside from the shock produced in some mainstream poetry readers at the time that a high art would dip so heavily into mass culture for its themes and subjects—given the New Critical decorum and moral seriousness at the time—there was the added impact of "offensive" erotic impulses and behaviors that O'Hara identifies with the film spectator. Much of the shock effect presumably derives from the recognition of how deep and personal the link between cinema and sexuality really is. Without O'Hara's blunt address of what occurs quite literally in the dark, the reader could blithely continue to accept the structures of forgetfulness, spectator passivity, and mass participation that render private experiences in the movie theater beyond reproach. With the Dean elegies, necrophilia is thrown into the mix of subversive sexual themes.

The identification—if not to say, obsession—of a gay poet with a male movie star is deeply bound up in O'Hara's efforts to make sense of himself as a rebel artist. He returned repeatedly to the movie theater to see *East of Eden*, and exchanged letters with Ashbery over who was more akin to the Dean character.[23] O'Hara immersed himself in Dean's brief career, and replays the facts of his premature death in a series of elegies for the star. "Thinking of James Dean" articulates the fantasy of how it would have been "had I died at twenty-four as he." The setting is pulled from the poet's sporadic theatrical career: "backstage / at the Brattle Theatre amidst the cold cream and the familiar lice / in my red-gold costume for a bit in *Julius Caesar*." By underscoring the material exigencies of the memory (cold cream and lice), O'Hara resists glamourizing his own fantasized early death. Nonetheless, he seizes the occasion to revisit his biography through this complex series of identifications, notably the truncated experiences in his own biography that link him to Dean, of having performed as a stage actor. O'Hara went so far as to write an "Ode on Necrophilia" that predates his writings on Dean.

This extremely brief poem begins with an epigraph from Palinurus: "Isn't there any body you want back from / the grave?" (*CP*, 280) The fact that the ode is traditionally employed to single out subjects worthy of praise in a public forum is, by now, a familiar aspect of O'Hara's loud, unapologetic redemption of culturally demoted subjects. The "any body" is a further offense to a public audience that would deny any participation in necrophiliac sentiments, for it is the *body* and not just the soul that is desirable to a self-diagnosed materialist sensibility such as O'Hara's. Necrophilia, as a societal danger, threatens an obsessive lust for the absent body that distracts from a healthy desire for surrounding bodies. This threat of non-reproductive sexual desire is only that much stronger when compounded thematically, as O'Hara dares, with the poet's gay identity.

Poetry magazine published "For James Dean" in March 1956, provoking an indignant letter in *Life* that the James Dean necrophilia had penetrated even the upper levels of culture." The most offensive stanza, as quoted by the letter, is the last:

> Men cry from the grave while they still live
> and now I am this dead man's voice,
> stammering, a little in the earth.
> I take up
> the nourishment of his pale green eyes,
> out of which I shall prevent
> flowers from growing, your flowers. (CP, 230)

O'Hara was attracted to the soft-spoken stammering charisma of Dean, as is evident in "Four Little Elegies." Not known to be at a loss for words himself, O'Hara's expression, "now I am this dead man's voice," conveys his pleasure at extending the after-life of a star in a society hostile to its disaffected, "useless" members. It also points to the structural make-up of the projections of his own "I" as effects produced by the incorporation of what is opposite and unlike himself into a hybrid, muted/voiced, absent/present, dead/living self in poetry: the trope of apostrophe worked out through the cinema. The poet's characterization of his work as full of "spleen, and ironically intimate observation" was inspired by his viewings of *East of Eden*. Irony and spleen come through especially in "For James Dean," which verges on hostility toward the fiercely competitive Hollywood: "Is it true that you high ones, celebrated / among amorous flies, hated the / prodigy and invention of his nerves?"

More threatening than the appropriation of a mass culture icon for poetry is the homoeroticism of a gay poet adopting the voice of this sexy icon of the counterculture. With "Four Little Elegies," O'Hara attempts the formal variety, emotive control, and public amplitude of Auden's "In Memory of W.B. Yeats." Whereas Auden's elegy has long achieved canonical status, O'Hara's poem, by virtue of his choice to elegize a young rebel movie star rather than a distinguished elder poet, shakes the cross-generational tradition of artistic inheritance. In the spring of 1955, Auden chose Ashbery over O'Hara as the Yale Series of Younger Poets prize recipient, criticizing the French influence especially in O'Hara's work. O'Hara's investment in distinguishing himself from Ashbery through the figure of James Dean, as well as his mention of Dean's admiration for French writers, such as Jean Genet and Colette, in "Four Little Elegies," may be clues to the double-edged challenge to Auden's celebrated elegy.

O'Hara's announced conversation is not with poetry, but with cinema, even as both media are obviously at play in terms of influence and inspiration for "Four Little Elegies." The second section of the poem, entitled "Little Elegy," is written in the loose, off-hand style that characterizes much of O'Hara's verse. Less successful than the beautiful elegiac poems of 1956, "In Memory of My Feelings" and "A Step Away From Them," "Little Elegy" invokes a self-consciousness over excessive mourning. States of mourning, like cinematically induced states, have the quality of being not quite real: "Let's cry a little while / as if we're at a movie / and not think of all life's / fun for a little while" (*CP*, 248). O'Hara's inclusion of the reader in the escapism promises that whatever might be considered elicit or taboo is placed front and center.

In "Obit Dean, September 30, 1955," the third of "Four Little Elegies," the emotional charge derives from the daring poetic maneuver of adapting the journalistic form of Dean's obituary to a life/death conversation with the movie actress Carole Lombard. Lombard died in a plane crash in 1942 on a trip to entertain American troops, so her role in the ode as stand-in for the classical Greek goddess, bears important affinities to the biographies (written and yet-to-be written) of these two young American men. A reading of the poem is haunted by the awareness that O'Hara is to follow Lombard and Dean to an early death in a fatal collision.

> OBIT DEAN, SEPTEMBER 30, 1955
>   Miss Lombard, this is a young
>   movie actor who just died
>   in his Porsche Spyder sportscar
>   near Paso Robles on his way
>   to Salinas for a race. This is
>   James Dean, Carole Lombard. I hope
>   you will be good to him up there.
>   He was not ill at all. He died
>   as suddenly as you did. He was
>   twenty-four. Although he acted first
>   on Broadway in *See the Jaguar,*
>   is perhaps best known for films
>   in which he starred: *East of Eden,*
>   *Rebel without a Cause* and *Giant.*
>   In the first of these he rocketed
>   to stardom, playing himself and us
>   "a brooding, inarticulate adolescent."
>
>   In New York today it's raining. If
>   there's love up there I thought that you
>   would be the one to love him. He's
>   survived by all of us, and so are you. (*CP*, 248–249)

Once again, as in "An Image of Leda," the key to O'Hara's identifications is the usage of the pronoun "us." In its first appearance—"playing himself and us"—we, the audience members, are cast as more or less interchange-able with the James Dean persona. As is widely acknowledged of this episode in American cinema, James Dean, like no one else, represents the disaffected, post-war youth: he represents "us." His life on and off screen achieves the heroic vulnerability of the "brooding, inarticulate adolescent" that for O'Hara is a desirable analogy to the rebel poet.

Through a clever, unusual use of pronouns, "us" appears for a second time at the end of the poetic obituary: "He's / survived by all of us, and so are you." The standard obituary phrase, "is survived by," is usually reserved for immediate family members. What does the poet add by this statement of the obvious, that *we* (the readers of the poem, the film audi-ence) are still alive? And to what purpose does the poem recall the address to Carole Lombard in the final phrase? I would propose that the reader is invited by the appearance of the final word, "you," to identify with the dead. The co-presence of "us" and "you" in the final line, far from clari-fying who is alive and who is dead, creates a slippage in the distinctions. O'Hara, by dwelling on the after-life of these two movie stars, and by seem-ingly pointing to our differences from them, invokes the after-life of the audience within the movie theater.

Whereas James Dean dies as a consequence of the risky lifestyle he rep-resents, we continue to watch and to take pleasure in the movies that sur-vive him. O'Hara includes in "Obit Dean" the fact that James Dean died before the release of his last two films. The result of this was that movie audiences had the eerie experience of watching the Dean character's near death in the car-racing dare of *Rebel Without a Cause* with the knowledge of his real death by car accident. By a near miss, it is the other adolescent, and not the Dean character, who rockets off a cliff. This near miss calls attention to how the film screen elides the actual presence of a person (or in this case, his absence) through the substitutive film presence. O'Hara's fascination with the off-screen persona and the on-screen effect is motivat-ed by his own projection of his out-of-poem life as an effect of an in-the-poem life. Our awareness that what we are watching is a remnant, a vestige, is brought to a stylistic crisis by the spectacle of Nicolas Ray's widescreen, color motion picture vehicle for this larger-than-life adolescent. Lombard, as the protective female actress, or maternal recipient of a boy of the cinema, at once deflects and increases the potential erotic charge of "Obit Dean, September 30, 1955." Although O'Hara addresses Lombard with a seemingly straight list of biographical facts about Dean's life and premature death, the poet does not entirely disguise his flare as self-interested matchmaker.

O'Hara was known among his friends for being attracted to men who were attracted to women, and the biography reports in O'Hara's frequent strategy of displacement through the woman in a love triangle (Gooch, 227). The investment in "Obit Dean" in conveying to Lombard the exact details and proper names that would seem to have little import in the face of death—from the "Porsche Spyder sportscar/ near Paso Robles" to the introduction of the *menage à trois*, "James Dean, Carole Lombard. I hope"—points to a self-conscious effort to underplay emotive and erotic feelings by way of biographical accuracy.

Written in the same period as "To the Film Industry in Crisis," the Dean elegies raise the stakes of O'Hara's dually ironic and enamored posture toward Hollywood. Daring a direct address of the immortalized movie stars, O'Hara personalizes the gap between spectator and screen. In response to the dominance of the moving image, O'Hara exhibits that the indifference of cinema—that it doesn't care— is liberating for personal self-expression. Ambivalence about the cinema, verging on fear and jealousy, because expressed in O'Hara's work, unlike that of most of his contemporaries, also becomes the point of departure for a positive embrace of how poetry is changed, and opened up, by it.

This does not mean that O'Hara does not enjoy making a few jabs about the salivating commercialism of cinema in which he participates. In "In Thinking of James Dean," O'Hara plays out the in-joke that to cinema-saturated America, even heaven is envisioned as a Hollywood star system. Here the analogy is to the vivid sensory effects of eighteenth and nine-teenth-century painters Tiepolo and Turner. O'Hara describes "the flush effulgence of a sky Tiepolo / and Turner had compiled in vistavision. / Each panoramic second of / his death" (*CP*, 230). Vistavision was fresh on movie screens in 1954, just the year before, and surely part of O'Hara's zeal for assimilating cinema into poetry is the feeling of being a novelty poet on the cutting edge of experience. Who, besides O'Hara, had the chance or the desire to write of Tiepolo and vistavision in the same breath, or to clock the moments following James Dean's death as "panoramic seconds"? Yet the formulations are apt. To a 1950s sensibility, exposed to the Hollywood cinema of the day, Tiepolo's exaggerated ceiling perspectives and Turner's sky canvases inevitably call forth associations with vistavision, just as the name "James Dean" is inseparable from his widescreen image.

Flirting with impossibilities, such as that Turner knew about cinema, or that Hollywood movie stars mingle in the afterlife, O'Hara exploits cinema's mind-bending logic of temporality. The powerful moving presence of cinema works across our expected temporal boundaries. James Dean vis-cerally appears, speaks, represents us, even as we know cognitively of his death. Recalling Comolli's point, "there is no spectator other than the one *aware* of the spectacle," it is worth assessing O'Hara's unique contribution of a poetic critique of film experience. By raising the "hidden" pleasures of film art into full view, and by converting what might be alienated, illicit experience into a liberating visual context for erotic identification and conversation with film stars, O'Hara renders the gap not only amorous, but verbal.

O'Hara took seriously his role as poet to describe the contemporary states of emotion and experience, perhaps most when his style seems flip, or his themes lowbrow. O'Hara assumes a *jouissance* at being in the heart of capitalist activity and the New York entertainment industry. Many in his circle of poet friends, Schuyler, Kenneth Koch, and Ginsberg among them, encouraged a comic, counter-cultural stance for serious contemporary poetry.[24] For O'Hara, the movie theater offered a materialist's dream of overproduction and endlessly proliferating stars, a circulating series of films old and new to choose from, and, what is more, a popular sensual experience which would be taboo as a serious subject for poets writing more recognizably within the tradition.

O'Hara's pledge of love in "To the Film Industry in Crisis" seizes upon how cinema continuously projects personality in the absence of actual persons. O'Hara's gesture is one of overcompensation for the paradox that cinema is a point of access to intense emotions that the medium itself lacks. O'Hara thus employs exalted adjectives, and converts cinema's impersonal technological features into love-worthy proper names. The command upon our attention is significantly emotional rather than visual. There is no attempt to recreate mimetically the effects of cinemascope or technicolor. But there is an appeal to our emotions that is recognizably immediate, vulgar, and full of effects of presence. O'Hara ends the poem with the ironic wish for the eternity of film stars:

> Long may you illumine space with your marvelous appearances, delays and enunciations, and may the money of the world glitteringly cover you as you rest after a long day under the kleig lights with your faces in packs for our edification, the way the clouds come often at night but the heavens operate on the star system. It is a divine precedent you perpetuate! Roll on, reels of celluloid, as the great earth rolls on! (*CP*, 232–233)

The invocation of the awesome natural realities of the stars, clouds, and earth, is the other, natural side of the hybrid equation with the vulgarity of glittering money, kleig lights, face-packs, and the artificial star system. This natural vulgarity is what O'Hara, despite the impersonality of the film industry, wants to posit as what is not beautiful, but *is* real. O'Hara finds this oxymoronic posture attractive because it enables him to launch himself as an empowered "I" through the disempowered life/art hybrid he finds himself in. To respond adequately and unblinkingly to the life side of the equation (the materialist concerns of his day and situation), as well as to push forward the artistic tradition he inherits, O'Hara draws from a techni-aesthetic model already in place: that of the cinema. O'Hara makes his appeal to an artificial Heaven, pivoting between "reels" and "reals," through the language effects of a technological sublime.

Afterword

The literal apparatus is situated as this project's model for a particular kind of reality effect, whether of visual or verbal reality. The postcard, the stereoscope, and 3-D cinema each produce effects of hyperrealism; the structural tendency of these apparatuses is toward effects that seem, however momentarily or partially, more real than reality. This is due to the photographic, mechanical reproduction of images, for which there is no equivalent technical development in the poetic medium. But even as poetry lacks a technical apparatus, it nonetheless has verbal means to generate analogous effects. The point of discussing the photographic apparatus in the context of poetic reality effects is that it highlights how the kind of hyperrealism shared by both media involves a displacement of art function.

Colored picture postcards, Rudolf Arnheim writes, "are not art and are not intended to be," but film (like painting, music, literature or dance) is a hybrid medium, for it is not necessarily art, but it can be. The failure of cinema to reproduce visual reality accurately, according to Arnheim, is what makes it art. He draws an analogy between the stereoscope and 3-D cinema to point out that three-dimensional depth perception is not natural to the medium of cinema: the principle of the stereoscope (based on binocular vision, where two photographs are taken at once, about the same distance apart as the human eyes) "cannot be used for film without recourse to awkward devices, such as colored spectacles" (Arnheim, 268–70). It is not possible to project an entirely stereoscopic film to an audience because of cinema's essentially two-dimensional character. This fact, for Arnheim, is crucial to film's status as art.

My emphasis is opposite to that of Arnheim's: to show where poetry attempts to efface itself as art by reproducing strategies learned from the postcard, the stereoscope, or 3-D cinema. The failure of this effacement, and the fact that poetry always half-retains its aesthetic status, is part of the effect. For lyric poetry is perhaps the least likely of artistic genres to prompt the question: is it art? Unlike narrative and dramatic verse, which rely to a certain extent upon plots of history, morality, heroism, and so on, lyric poetry's principal concern is with the aesthetic expression of personal emotion. The isolation of the aesthetic in the form of sensory effects, in the nineteenth-century lyric poetry of Keats and Dickinson, or Baudelaire and Rimbaud, generates intersense effects of synaesthesia. I am interested in the phenomenon of poetic synaesthesia in the twentieth century because of its hybrid status: a pure concentration of art function, on the one hand, and the sensation of reality, on the other.

I have pointed to Stevens, Bishop, and O'Hara as poets who are each concerned with effects of synaesthesia. And these sensory effects, to the extent that they aspire to be more real than reality, involve a structural displacement of the verbal medium. In order to circulate between the senses, not just between words, but for real, the poets attempt to bypass their verbal medium. This is impossible, but the effort is nonetheless to have words operate *as* senses: not merely to describe, but actually to perceive and to feel one sense modality in terms of another.

The relation between sense modalities that is most significant for twentieth-century American poets is that between sight and touch. This is due to the growth of image technologies, beginning already in the early nineteenth century, but gaining force and acceleration in the twentieth century, that accentuate the gap between reality as tangible and reality as visual. Jonathan Crary writes in *Techniques of the Observer* not of a dissociation between the individual and the perceptible world, but of a dissociation across the senses. Crary focuses on the separation of sight from touch, locating a new mode of decorporealized vision in technological changes of the 1830s and 40s.

> The loss of touch as a conceptual component of vision meant the unloosening of the eye from the network of referentiality incarnated in tactility and its subjective relation to perceived space. . . . Not only did the empirical isolation of vision allow its quantification and homogenization but it also enabled the new objects of vision (whether commodities, photographs, or the act of perception itself) to assume a mystified and abstract identity, sundered from any relation to the observer's position within a cognitively unified field. (Crary, 19)

Technologies of perception mark the emergence of a modern viewing subject: at the interface of perception and technology, the eye is severed from the tactility of the body. Instruments such as the camera obscura and the stereoscope intensify the accuracy of the eye while negating the capacity to touch what is seen. This is a paradoxical mode of vision, in which the act of seeing has embedded within it the negation of a tangible field of reference. A crisis over what the "object" is or can be follows from this negation of referential certitude.

The effort to navigate this crisis through poetry is always a self-effacing one, because language is foreclosed from both the sensual and the visual, touch and sight. I observed above that twentieth-century sensory effects of the real involve a displacement of art function, and this is true whether the medium is principally visual or verbal. The literal apparatus foregrounds this displacement, as in the examples of the hand-held postcard as visible token of what is tangibly absent, the stereoscopic image of an artificially three-dimensional view, and the 3-D emergence of a hand from the movie screen. In lyric poetry, the displacement of art function is not so immediately, and materially, evident: how can poetry cease to be art, by virtue of its reality effects?

Recall Susan Stewart's point that "when language attempts to describe the concrete, it is caught in an infinitely self-effacing gesture of inadequacy, a gesture which speaks to the gaps between our modes of cognition—those gaps between the sensual, the visual, and the linguistic" (Stewart, 52). The gap between the sensual and the visual is the one to which modern synaesthetic poetry speaks. And the crucial point is that poetry cannot help but speak, even when it is pretending not to, or when it is addressing a gap (as between touch and sight) in which language is not involved.

What the poets each know is that the aesthetic aspect of lyric poetry is irrepressible, even when the medium is manipulated to address a reality function that seems antipathetic to art. Stevens sets this up by his poetry of negative synaesthesia: the reader experiences sense as the absence of any particular sense. In Stevens, the evening out of the senses, as in the example "To see / To hear, to touch, to taste, to smell, that's now, / That's this" (CP, 225), is a blockage of seeing a particular image, hearing a given sound, or touching a material object. This is not the absence of all sensation, for what *is* left are the names for each category of sense. The artificiality of the names for sensing ("to see . . .to touch"), as well as the taxonomic divisions between the five senses, are proffered as their own positive experience. The crucial paradox is that these verbal reality effects pretend to be a rarefied form of the aesthetic, even as they are radically displacing of the aesthetic.

For Bishop, the failed efforts to materialize poetry into a literal apparatus—to bypass artificiality—produces its own verbal reality. Bishop's efforts work against poetic logic to render things visible to the point of tangibility. She writes in "Poem" of her uncle's miniature painting, "how touching in detail." Poetic images seemingly take on three-dimensionality through her linguistic apparatus. Like Barthes' punctum, her isolated, aesthetic, concrete details seem to emerge tangibly from out of a photo-realistic surface or frame. Likewise in O'Hara, his hybrid techni-aesthetic addresses the gap between sight and touch. I have staged his two poles as the real, tangible spectator and the visible, untouchable film star; the third dimension is that of the poems themselves. O'Hara's synaesthetic effects and claims to hyperreality are both undermined by and dependent upon the fact that his poetic medium is artificial, but aesthetic rather than techno-logical in character.

The denial of art function in the poets' attempts to appropriate the deno-tative structure of the technical, visual apparatus, is a failed one. And this is the heart of the linguistic paradox of intersense exchange. The attempt to bypass the verbal medium as construct, and to produce actual effects when there are none, has the paradoxical effect of calling attention to the verbal apparatus in the same gesture that it effaces it. Synaesthesia, the height of aesthetic stylization, is also at odds with artistic function. It reproduces the structure of the literal apparatus in which the stronger the illusion of actual sensation, the stronger the awareness of that sensation as a construct. Just when the reader imagines an experience of synthesis, and of a wholeness of reality, is when that reality is revealed as partial, con-structed, made of words rather than sense.

Notes

NOTES TO INTRODUCTION

[1] Walter Benjamin, "The Work of Art in the Age of Mechanical Reproduction" *Illuminations*, Trans. Harry Zohn (New York: Schocken Books, 1968), 217–251.

[2] Gertrude Stein, *Tender Buttons* in *Selected Writings of Gertrude Stein* (New York: Vintage, 1990), 459–509.

[3] Robert Frost, "The Master Speed," *Complete Poems of Robert Frost* (New York, Chicago, and San Francisco: Holt, Rinehart and Winston, 1964), 392.

[4] Martin Heidegger, "What are Poets For?" *Poetry, Language, Thought*, Trans. Albert Hofstadter (New York: Harper & Row Publishers, 1971), 91–142. Also, "The Question Concerning Technology," *The Question Concerning Technology and Other Essays*, Trans. William Lovitt (New York: Harper & Row Publishers, 1977) 3–49.

[5] Charles Baudelaire, *The Painter and Modern Life and Other Essays*, Trans. Johnathan Mayne (Greenwich: Phaidon, 1964).

[6] Charles Altieri, "Eliot's Impact on Twentieth-Century Poetry," *The Cambridge Companion to T.S. Eliot*. Ed. A. David Moody. (Cambridge: Cambridge University Press, 1994), 204–7.

[7] Jonathan Crary, *Suspensions of Perception: Attention, Spectacle, and Modern Culture* (Cambridge, MA and London: MIT Press, 2001).

[8] Rudolf Arnheim, *Film As Art* (Berkeley and Los Angeles: University of California Press, 1954).

[9] T.S. Eliot, *On Poetry and Poets* (London: Faber and Faber, 1957).

[10] Jerome McGann, *Black Riders: The Visible Language of Modernism* (New Jersey: Princeton University Press, 1993); Charles Altieri, *Painterly Abstraction in Modernist American Poetry* (Cambridge, Eng.: Cambridge University Press, 1989).

[11] Marjorie Perloff, *Radical Artifice: Writing Poetry in the Age of Media* (Chicago: University of Chicago Press, 1991).

[12] Perloff, *Frank O'Hara: Poet Among Painters* (Chicago: University of Chicago Press, 1998); "Revolving in Crystal: The Supreme Fiction and the Impasse of Modernist Lyric," in Albert Gelpi, ed., *Wallace Stevens: The Poetics of Modernism* (Cambridge: Cambridge University Press, 1985), 41–64.

[13] Carrie Noland, *Lyric Aesthetics and the Challenge of Technology* (New Jersey: Princeton University Press, 1999).

[14] Michael Davidson, *Ghostlier Demarcations: Modern Poetry and the Material Word* (Berkeley: University of California Press, 1997).

[15] Roland Barthes, *Camera Lucida: Reflections on Photography*. Trans. Richard Howard (New York: Noonday Press, 1981); *The Pleasure of the Text*. Trans. Richard Miller (New York: Hill and Wang, 1976).

[16] Rosalind Krauss, *The Optical Unconscious* (Cambridge, MA: MIT Press, 1994), 112.

[17] Walter Benjamin, "Little History of Photography," *Walter Benjamin: Selected Writings*, Vol. 2, 1927–1934, Trans. Rodney Livingstone (Cambridge, MA: The Belknap Press of Harvard University Press, 1999), 507–530.

[18] Michael Fried, "Between Realisms: From Derrida to Manet," *Critical Inquiry* 21: (Autumn 1994): 1–36.

[19] James Elkins, *What Painting Is* (New York: Routledge, 1999).

[20] W.J.T. Mitchell, "Ekphrasis and the Other," *Picture Theory: Essays on Verbal and Visual Representation* (Chicago: University of Chicago Press, 1994), 151–181. For scholarly background in ekphrasis, see Jean Hagstrum, *The Sister Arts: The Tradition of Literary Pictorialism and English Poetry From Dryden to Gray* (Chicago: University of Chicago Press, 1958), Murray Krieger, "The Ekphrastic Principle and the Still Moment of Poetry; or *Laokoon* Revisited," in *The Play and Place of Criticism* (Baltimore: Johns Hopkins University Press, 1967), and Wendy Steiner, *The Colors of Rhetoric: Problems in the Relation Between Modern Literature and Painting* (Chicago: University of Chicago Press, 1982).

[21] Wallace Stevens, *Letters of Wallace Stevens*, ed. Holly Stevens (Berkeley: University of California Press, 1966), 797; Elizabeth Bishop, *Elizabeth Bishop: One Art, Letters, Selected and Edited*, ed. Robert Giroux (New York: Farrar, Straus, Giroux, 1994),114–116; Brad Gooch, *City Poet: The Life and Times of Frank O'Hara* (New York: Harper, 1993), 221.

[22] Examples include Stevens fending off his wife's return so he could be alone with the new piano; Bishop moving her bulky clavier between storage places and homes; O'Hara writing musical compositions on bunk beds in the Navy. In the last decade, books have been written on each of the poets' connections with painting, painters, and the visual. By expanding the visual to include technology, I stretch the mimetic model of visual-verbal relation that I take to be a limitation in each of the books, even as mimesis is a subject of critique in each: Glen MacLeod, *Wallace Stevens and Modern Art: From the Armory Show to Abstract Impressionism* (New Haven: Yale University Press, 1993); Bonnie Costello, *Elizabeth Bishop: Questions of Mastery* (Cambridge, MA: Harvard University Press, 1991); Perloff, *Frank O'Hara*.

[23] Elaine Scarry, *Dreaming by the Book* (New York: Farrar, Straus & Giroux, 1999); Peter Schwenger, *Fantasm and Fiction: On Textual Envisioning (Cultural Memory in the Present)* (Stanford: Stanford University Press, 1999).

NOTES TO CHAPTER I

[1] Wallace Stevens, *Letters of Wallace Stevens*, ed. Holly Stevens (Berkeley: University of California Press, 1966), 629; hereafter abbreviated *L*.

² Stevens fostered multiple correspondences with people he was never to meet; in the case of McGreevy, the two men were not to meet until five years later. He would announce the entrance of a new correspondent into his collection, emphasizing their connection to a particular city or region: "I have a new correspondent, a citizen of Dublin" (*L*, 599).

³ Stevens claimed to deride "large views of things, like photographs of lakes and mountains from the terraces of chateaux" as a form of "intellectual tourism" (*L*, 601), seeking the genuine flavor of a place by more intimate means. Such views, however, were often precisely the ones sent by his friends abroad.

⁴ A large number of the items Stevens solicited came through his longstanding contact with the Parisian bookseller, M. Vidal, followed by the daughter, Paule Vidal. He wrote to the latter in 1953: "After waiting for FIGARO a long time, several numbers came at the same time. This has brought Paris close to me. When I go home at night, after the office, I spend a long time dawdling over the fascinating phrases which refresh me as nothing else could. I am one of the many people around the world who live from time to time in a Paris that has never existed and that is composed of the things that other people, primarily Parisians themselves, have said about Paris. That particular Paris communicates an interest in life that may be wholly fiction, but, if so, is a precious fiction" (*L*, 773).

⁵ "By gypsy cards, I do not mean the ones specifically gypsy, but all of them as tokens of your wandering. I have often seen Seville before but never smelled the heavy fragrance of its orange blossoms. And I have seen Granada but never felt the noise of its mountain water. Also, I have been in Madrid but this time it was a change to get away from the prado and to go to restaurants and sit by the door and look out at the 18ᵗʰ century. I liked to stop at Bordeaux where other friends of mine have lived" (*L*, 837).

⁶ See Roland Barthes, "The Photographic Message," and "Rhetoric of the Image," in *Image-Music-Text*, trans. Stephen Heath (New York: Hill and Wang, 1982), as well as the late, exceptional, *Camera Lucida*.

⁷ In one photo-postcard of Chelsea Sqaure, Stevens penned in an arrow to show his New York apartment building at 441 West Twenty-first Street. The postcard prompts such literal indexing of the sender's location, even as the arrowing calls attention to the sender's absence. Reprinted in Joan Richardson, *Wallace Stevens: A Biography*, Vol. I (New York: Beech Tree Books, 1986), 384i.; hereafter abbreviated in text as Richardson.

⁸ From *The Collected Poems of Wallace Stevens* by Wallace Stevens, copyright 1954 by Wallace Stevens and renewed 1982 by Holly Stevens, p. 485–6. Used by permission of Alfred A. Knopf, a division of Random House, Inc. Hereafter abbreviated *CP*.

⁹ Naomi Schor, "*Cartes Postales*: Representing Paris 1900," *Critical Inquiry* 18 (Winter 1992): 200; hereafter cited as Schor.

¹⁰ Ancu Rosu, *The Metaphysics of Sound in Wallace Stevens* (Tuscaloosa: University of Alabama Press, 1995), 72; hereafter cited in text as Rosu.

¹¹ Alan Filreis, *Wallace Stevens and the Actual World* (Princeton: Princeton University Press, 1991), 207–241.

¹² Vendler extends an analysis of desire and despair across her readings of the long poems, as well as in a slender critical volume on Stevens' shorter poems. See *On Extended Wings: Wallace Stevens' Longer Poems* (Cambridge, MA: Harvard

University Press, 1969) and *Wallace Stevens: Words Chosen Out of Desire* (Cambridge: Harvard University Press, 1984); the latter hereafter cited in text as Vendler, *Desire*. Bloom casts Stevens in a lineage of British and American romantic crisis-poetry in *The Poems of Our Climate* (Ithaca: Cornell University Press, 1977). Lisa Steinman, *Made in America: Science, Technology, and American Modernist Poets* (New Haven: Yale University Press, 1987).

[13] Among the analyses of Stevens' relation to modern painters, ranging from Cézanne to Mondrian, Altieri's philosophically speculative book is most pertinent for its chapter on "Why Stevens Must Be Abstract," which overlaps in its close readings with two poems I consider here, "Large Red Man Reading" and "An Ordinary Evening in New Haven." MacLeod's is a useful sourcebook for the rich field of Stevens' biographical affiliations with painters, contemporary visual art, and journals of art theory. Costello makes an important step toward casting the relation, in Stevens' terms, as one of analogy rather than imitation, in her "Wallace Stevens and Painting" in Albert Gelpi, ed., *Wallace Stevens: The Poetics of Modernism* (Cambridge: Cambridge University Press, 1985). An earlier step is made by Michael Benamou in *Wallace Stevens and the Symbolist Imagination* (Princeton: Princeton University Press, 1972), but his link between Stevens and French Impressionism, rather than Cubism, Fauvism, or another variant of distinctly modernist art, is now generally viewed as a wishful comparison.

[14] Evidence of Stevens' interests includes his visit to the Armory Show in 1913, his friendships with the artists of the New York Arensburg Circle, and his prose writings on painting and poetry in *The Necessary Angel: Essays on Reality and the Imagination* (New York: Vintage, 1951) and *Opus Posthumous: Poems, Plays, Prose*, ed., Milton J. Bates (New York: Vintage, 1989).

[15] Stevens writes to McGreevy on October 24, 1952, "Your reference to the cliffs of Moher caught my eye, since Jack Sweeney had sent me a photographic postcard of these rocks which I had placed in my room where I could see it" (*L*, 762) He also wrote to Barbara Church: "Jack Sweeney . . . sent me a photograph of the Cliffs of Moher in Ireland last summer which eventually became a poem" (*L*, 769–70), in a variation of an earlier note to Church, "Jack Sweeney (the Boston Sweeney) sent me a post-card from County Clare the other day—the worn cliffs towering up over the Atlantic. It was like a gust of freedom, a return to the spacious solitary world in which we used to exist . . . I hope you will not find this letter 'illisible.' " (*L*, 760–1) Note the number of references to seeing, and the punning on visibility and legibility. Jacques Derrida draws affinities between the letter and the postcard along the lines of legibility: "letters are always post cards: neither legible nor illegible, open and radically unintelligible." *The Post Card: From Socrates to Freud and Beyond*. Trans. Alan Bates (Chicago, 1987), 79.

[16] Here the "Word" substitutes for the "Photograph" with the violence that Barthes ascribes to the photograph: "The Photograph is violent: not because it shows violent things but because on each occasion *it fills the sight by force*, and because nothing in it can be refused or transformed," *Camera Lucida*, 91.

[17] Ernst Gombrich makes the arguable point in *Art and Illusion* that the impulse for visual resolution at the site of ambiguity is such that "we will [never see] an appearance of uncertain meaning." Part of what it means to have the capacity for perception is to have the need for something to take visual shape and form: "to perceive means to guess at something somewhere, and this need will persist even when we are presented with some abstract configuration where we lack the guidance of

previous experience" *Art and Illusion: A Study in the Psychology of Pictorial Illusion* (Oxford: Phaidon Press, Fifth Edition, 1977), 258.

[18] Harold Bloom, *The Poems of Our Climate* (Ithaca, N.Y.: Cornell University Press, 1977), 307.

[19] Edmund Burke, "Of Words" in *A Philosophical Inquiry into the Origin of Our Ideas of the Sublime and Beautiful* (New York, 1844), 206–7.

[20] Eleanor Cook, *Poetry, Word-Play, and Word-War in Wallace Stevens* (New Jersey: Princeton University Press, 1988), 301; hereafter abbreviated in text as Cook.

[21] The peculiar inseparability of the two faces of the postcard poses the collector with a dilemma; Benjamin notes the conflict between stamp and postcard collecting: "Sometimes you come across stamps on postcards and are unsure whether you should detach them or keep the card as it is, like a page by an old master that has different but equally precious drawings on both sides," "One-Way Street" in *Walter Benjamin: Selected Writings*, Vol. 1, (Cambridge, MA: The Belknap Press of Harvard University Press, 1996), 478.

[22] The Wallace Stevens Collection of the Huntington Library, WAS 150, San Marino, California.

[23] The postcard was followed that winter by a letter from McGreevy: "Of the nights nothing, neither content nor discontent but just going to bed with the assumption that I and the Roman morning would be together again in the course of a few hours." Reprinted in George Lensing, *Wallace Stevens: A Poet's Growth* (Baton Rouge and London: Louisiana State University Press, 1986), 9; Lensing's chapter on "Correspondence" addresses some of the same materials of Stevens' late correspondence and is a useful introduction to the poet's affair with foreign places.

[24] The postcard was threatening to the upper classes in its early days because of its potential infringement on the privacy of communication (Schor, 210). Stevens received much of his correspondence at his office in Hartford, prompting his friend Walter Pach to send one postcard (an Italian Easter greeting with children popping out of egg-shell train cars) in an envelope for fear of shocking the insurance-company employees. The postcard is reprinted in Richardson, Vol. 1, 384i.

[25] Walter Benjamin, "Unpacking My Library: A Talk About Book Collecting," *Illuminations*, trans. Harry Zohn, ed. Hannah Arendt (New York, 1968), 60.

[26] The eleven sections of the poem, reprinted in *Selected Poems*, ed. Samuel French Morse (New York: Vintage Books, 1959), fall in the following order: I, VI, IX, XI, XII, XVI, XXII, XXVIII, XXX, XXXI, XXIX.

[27] The famous Elm Street in New Haven underscores this connection.

[28] Gaston Bachelard, *The Poetics of Reverie*. Trans. Daniel Russell. (Boston: Beacon Press, 1969), 115.

[29] The debut of the first American picture postcards was in 1893, at the World's Columbian Exposition in Chicago. With the division of the postcard's back in 1904, split between message and address, came a rise of the primacy of the illustrated side of the card. A postcard of the Fordham Heights boarding house where Stevens was taking meals, dated March 7, 1907, still reserves one side for the address, and the other side for the photograph and a marginal message. Stevens pencilled in an arrow to show his bedroom window, and wrote next to image: "This is a picture of the house in which I take my meals." In its early stages, prior to the regularization of the postcard, Stevens was presumably one of many to let the ver-

bal message spill over onto the other side of the card, despite the explicit inscription THIS SIDE FOR THE ADDRESS. This practice of treating the postcard like unusual stationary, a letter-postcard hybrid, is still common, although somewhat subversive insofar as it negates the commercial status of the free-standing postcard. Reproduced in Richardson, *Vol. 1*, 192.

[30] Elaine Scarry, "On Vivacity: The Difference Between Daydreaming and Imagining-Under-Authorial-Instruction" *Representations* 52 (Fall 1995): 17.

[31] Susan Stewart, *Narratives of the Miniature, the Gigantic, the Souvenir, the Collection* (Durham: Duke University Press, 1993), 52; hereafter cited in text as Stewart.

[32] Ernst Gombrich explains that part of what it means to have the capacity for perception is to have the need for something to take visual shape and form: "to perceive means to guess at something somewhere, and this need will persist even when we are presented with some abstract configuration where we lack the guidance of previous experience" *Art and Illusion: A Study in the Psychology of Pictorial Representation* (Oxford: Phaidon Press, 1977), 258. See also James Elkins' *The Object Stares Back: On the Nature of Seeing* (New York: Simon and Schuster, 1996).

[33] See Stevens' poem, "The Planet on the Table," for an implicit alliterative slippage between poem and planet.

[34] Dee Reynolds' discussion of sites of imaginary space in Mallarmé is pertinent to the reading of Stevens: "The reader is invited to engage in imagining activity through the continuous making and remaking of images. . . . Paradoxically, the overwhelming sense of emptiness is not conveyed in abstract terms: it is the sensation of the Void which emerges through these shadowy, abstract, presences." *Symbolist Aesthetics and Early Abstract Art: Sites of Imaginary Space* (Cambridge, Eng.: Cambridge University Press, 1995), 96–7.

[35] Altieri observes of the poem that reading "shifts the burden of language from representation to representativeness, from objective statements to potentially transpersonal functions." 355.

[36] Holly Stevens, "Holidays in Reality," printed in *Wallace Stevens: A Celebration*, eds. Frank Doggett and Robert Buttel. (Princeton: Princeton University Press, 1980), 105–113.

[37] A separate volume of letters exists for the correspondence between Stevens and José Rodríguez-Feo, *Secretaries of the Moon: The Letters of Wallace Stevens and José Rodriguez-Feo*, eds. Beverly Coyle and Alan Filreis (Durham: Duke University Press, 1986)

[38] Reproduction of the postcard, back and front, in Richardson, *Vol. 2*, 128i.

[39] "Discourse in a Cantina at Havana, "*Broom*, V (November 1923), 201–03. Reprinted as "Academic Discourse at Havana," *Hound and Horn*, III, (Fall 1929): 53–6; *CP*, 142–5.

[40] Dorathea Beard, "A Modern Ut Pictura Poesis: The Legacy of Fauve Color and the Poetry of Wallace Stevens," *The Wallace Stevens Journal* 8.1 (Spring 1984): 13.

[41] Michael Taussig, *Mimesis and Alterity: A Particular History of the Senses* (New York: Routledge, 1993), 57.

[42] T.V.F. Brogan and Alfred Engstrom, *The New Princeton Handbook of Poetic Terms* (Princeton: Princeton University Press, 1994), 301.

[43] I. A. Richards, *Principles of Literary Criticism* (London: Kegan Pual, Trench, Trubner, 1924).

[44] Stevens alludes to Baudelaire's idea of a "fundamental aesthetic" in his essay on "The Relations Between Poetry and Painting" in *The Necessary Angel* (New York: Vintage Books, 1990), 160.

[45] *Concordance to the Poetry of Wallace Stevens* (University Park, PA: Pennsylvania State University Press, 1963).

[46] Charles Altieri,"Wallace Stevens' Metaphors of Metaphor: Poetry as Theory" *American Poetry 1* (Fall 1983): 27–48.

[47] Hollander, "The Sound of Music and the Music of Sound," printed in Frank Doggett and Robert Buttel, eds., *Wallace Stevens: A Celebration*, 248.

[48] This passage is preceded in the letter to Barbara Church, August 9, 1948, by "Aix-en-Provence" standing in synecdoche for the whole of South of France, and additionally, for an apolitical sense of peace and security: "Does the South of France mean Aix-en-Provence? Except for the fact that one must remain forever on one's guard now, day and night, ready to grapple with the enticements of communism, how easy it would be, at Aix . . . to find a peace, a security, a sense of good fortune and of things that change only slowly . . ." (*L*, 609). In another letter, Stevens lets it be known that he is thinking of "Aix" as the literal "X" that marks the spot: "I envy every foot of the trip through France. On my death there will be found carved on my heart, along with the initials of lots of attractive girls, that I have known, the name of Aix-en-Provence" (*L*, 671).

[49] "Ode to a Nightingale," *John Keats*, (Oxford: Oxford University Press, 1990).

NOTES TO CHAPTER II

[1] "In the Village," Robert Giroux, ed. *Elizabeth Bishop, The Collected Prose* (New York: Farrar, Straus & Giroux, 1984), 225; hereafter abbreviated in the text as *Prose*.

[2] *Robert Lowell, Selected Poems* (New York: Farrar, Straus and Giroux, 1975),114.

[3] Cited in Bonnie Costello, *Elizabeth Bishop: Questions of Mastery* (Cambridge, MA: Harvard University Press, 1991), 37.

[4] Bishop's interest in Stevens was already established in the early 1930s at Vassar, when she claimed to know the 1931 edition of *Harmonium* almost by heart. She read *Ideas of Order* (1935) and *The Man with the Blue Guitar* (1937) with pleasure and interest when they came out, although expressed to Marianne Moore, who published a review of Stevens' *Poetry* which Bishop admired, that her own "ideas" about Stevens had her "wandering around them in the dark." (December 5, 1936 in Elizabeth Bishop, *One Art: Letters,* ed. Robert Giroux (New York: Farrar, Straus, & Giroux, 1994), 48. The Stevens-Bishop link has become a common canonical line in studies of American poetry. Among recent articles are Bonnie Costello's "Narrative Secrets, Lyric Openings: Stevens and Bishop," *The Wallace Stevens Journal* 19.2 (Fall 1995): 180–200, and Susan McGabe's "Stevens, Bishop, and Ashbery: A Surrealist Lineage," *The Wallace Stevens Journal* 22.2 (Fall 1998): 149–68.

[5] Elizabeth Bishop, *The Complete Poems* 1927–1979 (New York: Farrar, Strauss and Giroux, 1991), 40; hereafter abbreviated in the text as *CP*.

[6] Cited in the standard biography of Bishop by Brett Millier, *Elizabeth Bishop: Life and the Memory of It* (Berkeley: University of California Press, 1993), 131.

[7] In the epigraph to *Geography III*, Bishop follows a series of questions and answers, quoted directly from an 1884 geography primer, with a related series of questions, this time without answers: "*In what direction is the Volcano? The Cape? The Bay? The Lake? The Strait? . . . .*" The poems placed first in the volume describe volcanoes and molten liquid as seen in photographs ("In the Waiting Room"), through binoculars ("Crusoe in England"), and from a plane ("Night City"), as if such geographically explosive points of reference at once threaten to erupt and are held at a visual distance by this media.

[8] "Prize Poet," *Atlantic* (August 1946): 148.

[9] There have been several gender studies in the last decade that treat Bishop's visual perspectives; see David Jarraway's work on Bishop's spectral lesbian poetics and Frank Lentricchia's take on femininity in Stevens, each formative in the development of my interpretation of duality.

[10] Quoted in Millier, 118.

[11] David Kalstone recognizes a certain mode of description in Bishop's implicit analogy with the camera obscura in "The Sea & Its Shore": "one that emphasizes receptivity, the image conceived and recorded as a prior creation rather than being deliberately framed by the intervening and active artist." Kalstone, *Becoming a Poet: Elizabeth Bishop with Marianne Moore and Robert Lowell* (New York: Farrar, Straus and Giroux, 1989) 60.

[12] Cited in Crary, *Techniques of the Observer: On Vision and Modernity in the Nineteenth Century* (Cambridge and London: MIT Press, 1995, 40; hereafter cited as Crary, *Techniques*.

[13] See Sir Isaac Newton's elaborate, tactile descriptions of the set-up of each experiment in *Opticks, or A Treatise of the Reflections, Refractions, Inflections & Colours of Light* (London: G. Bell & Sons, 1931). The solitary pleasure in the details of making, against the backdrop of the narrator's effacement, invites comparison with Daniel Defoe's *Robinson Crusoe*, published 1717, as explored in this chapter's final section.

[14] In focusing on the bodilessness at the center of the epistemological model of the camera, Crary develops a critical strategy of recuperating what is not present to the eye, even as the technical instruments focus exclusively on what the eye sees, in Crary, *Techniques*, 40–53.

[15] David Lehman, "'In Prison': A Paradox Regained," printed in Lloyd Schwartz and Sybil P. Estess, eds., *Elizabeth Bishop and Her Art* (Ann Arbor: University of Michigan Press, 1983), 296; hereafter abbreviated in notes as *Her Art*.

[16] Bishop noted the changes World War II brought to Key West, ambivalently both regretting them and wishing to be part of the war effort. Her job at the Navy's binocular factory was a way to bring many of her fantasies to literal fruition: the requirements of a practical work place, the feeling of being needed by contemporary society, and her sense of technical, optical instruments as a means to controlling ambiguity. For a treatment of Bishop's feelings about the war, see Millier, 86–185.

[17] September 1, 1943; reprinted in Robert Giroux, ed., *Elizabeth Bishop: One Art, Letters, Selected and Edited* (New York: Farrar, Straus, Giroux, 1994), 114–116.

[18] The half-unlivable fantasies that frequent Bishop's oeuvre are often absurdly meant for living. Her biography attests to how she would make the same mistake over and over, living in homes she found too isolated or uncomfortable, in Florida, Maine, Brazil and elsewhere, obviously in an effort to realize her fantasy. Her attraction to Stevens' fantasy of living in a houseboat was genuine. Millier observes insightfully of "The End of March" that "the impossible 'proto . . . crypto' dream house brings to a close the poet's lifelong preoccupation with places of refuge, shelters, and solitary retreats,"491.

[19] Anne Stevenson, *Elizabeth Bishop* (New York: Twayne, 1966), 66.

[20] See the chronology of essays and reviews in *Her Art*.

[21] Lee Edelman, "The Geography of Gender: Elizabeth Bishop's 'In the Waiting Room'" *Contemporary Literature*, 26, no. 2 (Summer 1985): 179–196. When trapped by critics with an error in the cited contents of the February 1918 issue, Bishop could but insist upon its accuracy nonetheless, and like the child persona cling more acutely to the facts before her "eye." The absurdity of this example, addressed by Edelman and others, suggests that for Bishop, the literal offers the only hinge against uncertainty; to undo the equation threatens too deeply the very notion of what is real.

[22] David Jarraway, "'O Canada!': The Spectral Lesbian Poetics of Elizabeth Bishop," *PMLA* 113 (March 1998), 249.

[23] Costello, *Elizabeth Bishop: Questions of Mastery* (Cambridge, MA: Harvard University Press, 1991).

[24] See Ashley Brown, "An Interview with Elizabeth Bishop," *Her Art*, 296.

[25] For a treatment of the theme of domesticity in Bishop's work, see Helen Vendler, "Domestication, Domesticity, and the Otherworldy" in *Her Art*, 32–48.

[26] Kaja Silverman, *The Threshold of the Visible World* (New York: Routledge, 1996), 129.

[27] Crary, *Technologies of the Observer*, 122–4.

[28] Holmes continues, describing a currency in images like that of bank-notes: "There is only one Colosseum or Pantheon; but how many millions of potential negatives have they shed—representatives of billions of pictures—since they were erected. Matter in large masses must always be fixed and dear; form is cheap and transportable. . . . There may grow up something like a universal currency of these bank-notes, or promises to pay in solid substance, which the sun has engraved for the great Bank of Nature." Oliver Wendell Holmes, "The Stereoscope and the Stereograph," in *Classic Essays on Photography*, ed. Alan Trachtenberg (New Haven: Leete's Island Books, 1980), 80–81.

[29] Costello, 229.

[30] Costello's comments on Bishop and Max Ernst's frottage methods are useful for understanding what is at work in the Bristol board: "In one sense frottage represents an extreme mimesis—art as a literal impression of nature, a sort of fossil, breaking down the distance between sign and thing, making the sign a literal trace of the thing," 222. Charles Peirce's theory of the indexical sign bears on the semiotic structures at play here, though for the sake of focus, I opt to frame Bishop's aesthetic approach to semiotics by way of Barthes rather than Peirce.

[31] Rosalind Krauss, in a discussion that at once treats the stereoscope and Max Ernst, addresses the optical logic of simultaneity, or "both-at-once," *The Optical Unconscious* (Cambridge, MA: The MIT Press, 1994), 209.

[32] Norman Bryson employs the term "hyperreality" in a discussion of sixteenth- and seventeenth-century still life artists, where mere realism is not sufficient: packed into the images of the humble, material objects of everyday life is a surplus of appearance, an excess of brilliance to focus all the senses—sight, smell, hearing, touch, taste. His account bears analogy with the sense-loaded images of the stereo-scope: Bryson, *Looking at the Overlooked: Four Essays on Still Life Painting* (Cambridge, MA: Harvard University Press, 1990), 62.

[33] Cited in Millier, 355.

[34] See Georg Simmel, "The Metropolis and Mental Life," trans. H.H.Gerth, in *Classic Essays on the Culture of Cities*, ed. Richard Sennett (Englewood Cliffs, N.J., 1969), 47–60.

[35] Poem #185, " 'Faith' is a fine invention," Emily Dickinson, *The Complete Poems of Emily Dickinson*, ed. Thomas Johnson (Boston: Little, Brown and Company, 1960), 87.

[36] Bishop writes in 1965, upon receiving Dr. Anny Baumann's gift of binoculars, "The world has wonderful details if you can get just a little closer than usual." Millier, 335.

[37] Mary McCarthy, New York Times Book Review (December 6, 1981), 68. Reprinted in *Bishop and Her Art*, 267.

[38] *Bishop and Her Art*, 285.

[39] Bishop wrote a postcard from her new Key West apartment, at 611 Francis Street, of a picture of Caribbean jewfish: "These are the *Fish*," Millier, 154; 208.

[40] Stevenson, 56.

[41] Elaine Scarry, "Imagining Flowers: Perceptual Mimesis (Particularly Delphinium)" *Representations* 57, (Winter 1997): 90–115.

[42] Thomas Travisiano, "'The Flicker of Impudence': Delicacy and Indelicacy in the Art of Elizabeth Bishop," Ed. Marilyn May Lombardi. *Elizabeth Bishop: The Geography of Gender* (Charlottesville: University Press of Virginia, 1993), 114.

[43] Lombardi, "The Closet of Breath," in *The Geography of Gender*, 63.

[44] Here Bishop hangs Harold Bloom, who claims for Bishop's famous eye, as for Dickinson's, that "what is most worth seeing is impossible to see, at least with open eyes," Introduction to Harold Bloom, ed., *Modern Critical Views: Elizabeth Bishop* (New York: Chelsea House Publishers, 1985), 2.

[45] A 1938 record of a dream likewise favors the size-scale of a fish over herself: "The fish was large, about 3 feet long, large—scaled, metallic like a goldfish only a beau-tiful rose color. I myself seemed slightly smaller than life-size." Millier, 117.

[46] David Jarraway, " 'O Canada!': The Spectral Lesbian Poetics of Elizabeth Bishop," *PMLA* 113 (March 1998): 249.

[47] Bishop's investment in solitude, in islands, in being figuratively ship-wrecked, in material treasures of her own making, in homosexual relations (as between Crusoe and Friday), and in survival based on minute details, all play into her interest in Crusoe. Bishop's work on Crusoe, which had been dormant, revived upon her visit to Darwin's house in Kent in the mid-1960s according to Millier, 367. One recalls her description of Darwin as the "lonely young man, his eyes fixed on facts and minute details . . .."

[48] Bishop's notion of the useless detail is akin to that employed by Barthes. Bishop had read some Barthes; see Marilyn May Lombardi, *The Body and the*

Song: Elizabeth Bishop's Poetics (Carbondale: Southern Illinois University Press, 1995), 70.

[49] What later reappears in *The Pleasure of the Text* and *Camera Lucida* as a pleasurable remainder or excess of meaning is accounted for in this essay as a resistance of meaning, and one that is cast as a visual-verbal breakdown. Barthes, "The Reality Effect," reprinted in Tzvetan Todorov, ed., *French Literary Theory Today: A Reader* (Cambridge: Cambridge University Press, 1982), 11.

[50] The detail challenges the hermeneutic assumptions by which we read. "What is at stake is nothing less than the legitimacy of the organic model of literary interpretation," comments Schor, "according to which all details—no matter how aberrant their initial appearance—can, indeed must be integrated into the whole, since the work of art is itself organically constituted." Schor, *Reading In Detail: Aesthetics and the Feminine* (New York: Routledge, 1987), 85.

[51] Martin Jay explores the experience of anxiety, and "trauma," with regard to the doubling of artifice and nature in the photograph/reality effect. He highlights the negativity of the effect to forward the argument that Barthes, among other French theorists, is engaged in a critique of ocularcentrism. *Downcast Eyes: The Denigration of Vision in Twentieth-Century French Thought* (Berkeley: University of California Press, 1993), 442.

[52] Barthes examines press photographs in an effort to separate denotation as much as possible from style and "second order" messages. Paradoxically, the artistic uselessness of Flaubert's details is collapsible with the pure functionalism of the press photograph, for they both lay bare denotative structure. Roland Barthes, "The Photographic Message," reprinted in *Image-Music-Text*, trans. Stephen Heath (New York: Hill and Wang, 1977), 18.

[53] Barthes, "The Reality Effect," 16.

[54] Schor, *Reading in Detail*, 87.

[55] "What I tire of so quickly in Wallace Stevens is the self-consciousness—poetry so aware lacks depth. Poetry should have more unconscious spots left in." Quoted in Lombardi, 178.

NOTES TO CHAPTER III

[1] Frank O'Hara, "Jackson Pollock," *Art Chronicles, 1954–1966* (New York: George Braziller, 1975), 32; hereafter abbreviated in text as *AC*. O'Hara also notes in this essay that Pollock chooses to use "no images with real visual equivalents," 34. The colors of Pollock's painting (yellow, ochre, black, blue-gray, violet, red-orange, white, and brown) foreground the painter's mixed palette, prompting O'Hara's association; the saturation of color in a technicolor sunset emphasizes cinematic style and spectacle over real visual equivalents.

[2] Many of the 1930s and 40s Technicolor films have subdued features that adhere to Hollywood norms of softness, low contrast, and diffusion, but the technology is identified nonetheless with excess and spectacle. David Bordwell, Janet Staiger, and Kristin Thompson, *The Classical Hollywood Cinema: Film Style and Mode of Production to 1960* (New York: Columbia University Press, 1985), 355.

[3] Yve-Alain Bois and Rosalind Krauss, *Formless: A User's Guide* (New York: Zone Books, 1997), 95.

[4] Printed in Frank O'Hara, *The Collected Poems*. Ed. Donald Allen (Berkeley and Los Angeles: University of California Press, 1995), 498–499, published with arrangement with Alfred A. Knopf; hereafter abbreviated in text as *CP*.

[5] "Oranges," O'Hara's series of twelve pastorals, were part of a collaboration exhibit with Grace Hartigan's paintings *Oranges*, at Tibor de Nagy gallery in April 1953. According to anecdote, O'Hara handed over the poems to Hartigan saying "How about a dozen oranges?" O'Hara's poems were copied, placed in thee ring hole binders, and sold at the show for a dollar each. Brad Gooch, *City Poet: The Life and Times of Frank O'Hara* (New York: HarperPerennial, 1993), 236; hereafter abbreviated as *Gooch*.

[6] Marjorie Perloff, *Frank O'Hara: Poet Among Painters* (Chicago: Chicago University Press, 1997), 112.

[7] Christian Metz, "Photography and Fetish," in *The Critical Image: Essays on Contemporary Photography*, ed. Carol Squiers (Seattle: Bay Press, 1990), 156.

[8] Perloff, *Frank O'Hara: Poet Among Painters*, 21.

[9] Helen Vendler, "Frank O'Hara: The Virtue of the Alterable," reprinted in Jim Elledge, ed., *Frank O'Hara: To Be True to a City* (Ann Arbor: The University of Michigan Press, 1990), 251.

[10] James Breslin, "Frank O'Hara" reprinted in Elledge, 253–298.

[11] John Ashbery, *Selected Poems* (New York: Penguin, 1985), 314–315.

[12] W.B.Yeats, "Leda and the Swan," *The Collected Poems of W.B. Yeats*, Ed. Richard J. Finneran, (New York: Macmillan Publishing Company, 1983), 215.

[13] Ashbery here refers to O'Hara's early work, but he places O'Hara in an "antiliterary and antiartistic" tradition characterized by attitudes of indifference. "Introduction" to O'Hara, *CP*, vii-xi. See also Marjorie Perloff, "Watchmen, Spy and Dead Man: Jasper Johns, Frank O'Hara, John Cage and the 'Aesthetic of Indifference'" *Modernism-Modernity* 2001 April 8: 2, 197–223.

[14] Christian Metz, "On the Impression of Reality in the Cinema" *Film Language: A Semiotics of the Cinema*, (Chicago: The University of Chicago Press, 1974), 9.

[15] Jean-Louis Comolli, "Machines of the Visible," printed in Teresa de Lauretis and Stephen Heath, eds., *The Cinematic Apparatus* (New York: St. Martin's Press, 1980), 121; hereafter abbreviated in text as Comolli.

[16] Bordwell, 358–9.

[17] John Ashbery writes: "The term 'New York School' applied to poetry isn't helpful, in characterizing a number of widely dissimilar poets whose work moreover has little to do with New York, which is, or used to be, merely a convenient place to live and meet people, rather than a specific place whose local color influences the literature produced there." Introduction to O'Hara, *CP*, x.

[18] Vendler's comment, that there is "no reason why a poem of this sort should ever stop," is linked to a concern that O'Hara introduces a style of writing that is antilyric and anti-poetic. Vendler, "Frank O'Hara: The Virtue of the Alterable," 235.

[19] Critic Laurence Goldstein notes how through 1960, poets writing about the popular arts went "against the grain of literary decorum," citing Yeats, Pound, Stevens, and Williams as poets who do not incorporate cinema in their verse, and providing commentary on poets who do, including Vachel Lindsay, Hart Crane, Delmore Schwartz, and Adrienne Rich, *The American Poet at the Movies: A Critical History* (Ann Arbor: University of Michigan Press, 1995)

[20] Charles Altieri, *Enlarging the Temple: New Directions in American Poetry During the 1960s* (Lewisburg, PA: Bucknell University Press, 1979), 108–22.

[21] Jim Elledge, "'Never Argue with the Movies': Love and the Cinema in the Poetry of Frank O'Hara," reprinted in Elledge, 350–7.

[22] John Ellis, "Stars as a Cinematic Phenomenon" printed in Gerald Mast, Marshall Cohen, and Leo Braudy, eds., *Film Theory and Criticism: Introductory Readings,* Fourth Edition (New York and Oxford: Oxford University Press, 1992), 614–621.

[23] O'Hara describes his affinities to James Dean in a letter to Fairfield Porter, a mutual friend of Ashbery's and O'Hara's: "that eerie feeling that I was being exposed to an intimate, scarcely-remembered level, whereas John identified with his brother . . . John's work is full of dreams and a kind of moral excellence and kind sentiments. Mine is full of objects for their own sake, spleen and ironically intimate observation which may be truthfulness (in the lyrical sense) but is more likely to be egotistical cynicism masquerading as honesty." Quoted in Gooch, 267–8.

[24] Both Ginsberg's *Howl* and O'Hara's elegies to James Dean appeared in 1955–6.

Bibliography

Altieri, Charles. *Painterly Abstraction in Modernist American Poetry and the Contemporaneity of Modernism.* Cambridge, Eng.: Cambridge University Press, 1989.

Arnheim, Rudolf. *Film As Art.* Berkeley: University of California Press, 1954.

Barthes, Roland. *Camera Lucida: Reflections on Photography.* Trans. Richard Howard. New York: The Noonday Press, 1981.

———. "The Reality Effect," in *French Literary Theory Today: A Reader.* Ed., Tzetvetan Todorov, Cambridge: Cambridge University Press, 1982.

Benjamin, Walter. "Little History of Photography," *Walter Benjamin: Selected Writings,* Vol. 2, 1927–1934. Cambridge, MA: The Belknap Press of Harvard University Press, 1996.

Bishop, Elizabeth. *The Collected Prose.* Ed. Robert Giroux. New York: The Noonday Press, 1984.

———. *The Complete Poems, 1927–1979.* New York: The Noonday Press, 1983.

———. *Elizabeth Bishop: One Art, Letters.* Ed. Robert Giroux. New York: Farrar, Straus, & Giroux, 1994.

Costello, Bonnie. *Elizabeth Bishop: Questions of Mastery.* Cambridge, MA: Harvard UP, 1991.

Crary, Jonathan. *Techniques of the Observer: On Vision and Modernity in the Nineteenth Century.* Cambridge, MA: MIT Press, 1995.

———. *Suspensions of Perception: Attention, Spectacle, and Modern Culture.* Cambridge, MA: MIT Press, 2001.

Davidson, Michael. *Ghostlier Demarcations: Modern Poetry and the Material Word.* 1997.

Derrida, Jacques. *The Post Card: From Socrates to Freud and Beyond.* Trans. Alan Bates. Chicago, 1987.

Drucker, Johanna. *Theorizing Modernism: Visual Art and the Critical Tradition.* New York: Columbia University Press, 1994.

Elkins, James. *What Painting Is.* New York: Routledge, 1999.

Elledge, Jim, ed. *Frank O'Hara: To Be True to a City.* Ann Arbor: The University of Michigan Press, 1990.

Fried, Michael. "Between Realisms: From Derrida to Manet." *Critical Inquiry* 21 (autumn 1994): 1–36.

Gombrich, Ernst. *Art and Illusion: A Study in the Psychology of Pictorial Illusion.* 5th ed. Oxford: Phaidon Press, 1977.

Gooch, Brad. *City Poet: The Life and Times of Frank O'Hara.* New York: Harper, 1993.

Heidegger, Martin. *The Question Concerning Technology and Other Essays.* Trans. William Lovitt. Cambridge: Cambridge University Press, 1994.

Jay, Martin. *Downcast Eyes: The Denigration of Vision in Twentieth-Century French Thought.* Berkeley: University of California Press, 1993.

Krauss, Rosalind. *The Optical Unconscious.* Cambridge, MA: The MIT Press, 1994.

⸻ and Bois, Yve-Alain. *Formless: A User's Guide.* New York: Zone Books, 1997.

MacLeod, Glen. *Wallace Stevens and Modern Art: From the Armory Show to Abstract Impressionism.* New Haven: Yale University Press, 1993.

McGann, Jerome. *Black Riders: The Visible Language of Modernism.* New Jersey: Princeton University Press, 1993.

Millier, Brett. *Elizabeth Bishop: Life and the Memory of It.* Berkeley: University of California Press, 1993.

Mitchell, W.J.T. *Picture Theory: Essays on Verbal and Visual Representation.* Chicago: University of Chicago Press, 1994.

Noland, Carrie. *Poetry at Stake: Lyric Aesthetics and the Challenge of Technology.* Princeton: Princeton University Press, 1999.

O'Hara, Frank. *Art Chronicles: 1954–1966.* New York: George Braziller, 1975.

⸻. *The Collected Poems of Frank O'Hara.* Ed. Donald Allen. Berkeley: University of California Press, 1995.

Perloff, Marjorie. *Frank O'Hara: Poet Among Painters.* Chicago: University of Chicago Press, 1998.

⸻. *Radical Artifice: Writing Poetry in the Age of Media.* Chicago: University of Chicago Press, 1991.

Reynolds, Dee. *Symbolist Aesthetics and Early Abstract Art: Sites of Imaginary Space.* Cambridge, Eng.: Cambridge University Press, 1995.

Richardson, Joan. *Wallace Stevens: A Biography.* 2 vols. New York: Beech Tree Books, 1988.

Scarry, Elaine. *Dreaming by the Book*. New York: Farrar, Straus & Giroux, 1999.

Schor, Naomi. "*Cartes Postales:* Representing Paris 1900" *Critical Inquiry* 18 (1992), 188–244.

———. *Reading in Detail: Aesthetics and the Feminine*. New York: Routledge, 1987.

Schwartz, Lloyd and Sybil Estess, eds. *Under Discussion: Elizabeth Bishop and Her Art*. Ann Arbor: The University of Michigan Press, 1983.

Schwenger, Peter. *Fantasm and Fiction: On Textual Envisioning (Cultural Memory in the Present)*. Stanford: Stanford University Press, 1999.

Stevens, Wallace. *The Collected Poems*. New York: Vintage, 1954.

———. *Letters of Wallace Stevens*. Ed. Holly Stevens. Berkeley: University of California Press, 1966.

———. *The Necessary Angel: Essays on Reality and the Imagination*. New York: Vintage, 1951.

———. *Opus Posthumous: Poems, Plays, Prose*. Milton J. Bates, ed. New York: Vintage, 1989.

Stewart, Susan. *Narratives of the Miniature, the Gigantic, the Souvenir, the Collection*. Durham: Duke University Press, 1993.

Taussig, Michael. *Mimesis and Alterity: A Particular History of the Senses*. New York: Routledge, 1993.

Index